KEYS TO INVESTING IN MUTUAL FUNDS

KEYS TO INVESTING IN MUTUAL FUNDS

Second Edition

Warren Boroson

Specialist Editor
The Record
Hackensack, New Jersey

All inquiries should be addressed to:
Barron's Educational Series, Inc.
250 Wireless Boulevard
Hauppauge, New York 11788

Library of Congress Catalog No. 91-30357

Library of Congress Cataloging Publication Data

Boroson, Warren.
    Keys to investing in mutual funds / Warren Boroson.—
2nd ed.
        p. cm.—(Barron's business keys)
    Includes index.
    ISBN 0-8120-4920-9
    1. Mutual funds. 2. Finance, Personal. I. Title. II. Series
HG4530.B67 1992
332.63'27—dc20   91-30357
                                                                      CIP

PRINTED IN THE UNITED STATES OF AMERICA
  45 9770 9876 .

ACKNOWLEDGMENTS

Author and publisher express their appreciation to the following
individuals and companies for permission to reprint material: Mary
C. Driscoll, Financial Planning Information; Richard P. Fried, Kanon
Bloch Carré & Co., Inc.; Joe Mansueto, Morningstar Inc.; Morgan,
Stanley & Company; Wiesenberger Investment Companies Service.

CONTENTS

INTRODUCTION

Mutual funds are, in some ways, like insurance.

With insurance, typically, a group of people band together to protect themselves against financial disaster. Each pays a sum of money into a pool, and should one of them suffer a calamity, that unfortunate will receive some of the money contributed by all the others. The calamity could be premature death, disability, disease, the loss of a major asset like a house.

With mutual funds, a group of people band together to make a greater profit than they might individually, and with greater safety. Because they can put more money into a fund by joining together, each member of the group can buy a piece of a wide mix of investments. Just as important, these funds are large enough to enable these people to hire top-flight professionals to manage those investments.

Of course, there are risks, but mutual funds have proven to be especially suitable for ordinary people — somewhat uninformed about investing, and wary, who normally confine themselves to low-return savings accounts or slightly higher-paying certificates of deposit. Such conservative investments will not make them rich — unless they save a great deal of money — and may not even keep their assets growing ahead of inflation.

With mutual funds, John and Jane Doe stand a far better chance of making more money — not just with money-market funds (which are like super checking accounts), but with fixed-income (bond) funds, and most especially with stock funds.

Turning a profit in the stock market can be a labor of Hercules for the average individual, as anyone who invested in the market shortly before the crash of 1987 knows all too well. But by investing in a good stock mutual fund, you turn the odds in your favor — and stocks, whether or not you know it, have been the safest and surest way (apart from owning a house) for the average investor to make a good deal of money.

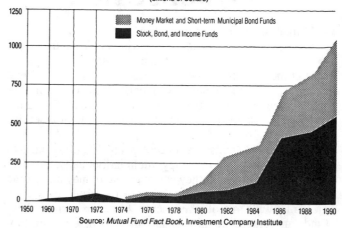

Assets of Mutual Funds
(billions of dollars)

Money Market and Short-term Municipal Bond Funds

Stock, Bond, and Income Funds

Source: *Mutual Fund Fact Book*, Investment Company Institute

Virtually all stock mutual funds lost money Black Monday. But mutual fund investors, by and large, lost much less of their portfolios' value than did most investors in individual stocks, some of whom were almost wiped out.

In short, with mutual funds you can diversify your investments for safety, meanwhile having a professional adviser decide which stocks to buy, which stocks to sell, and when. You don't need a minimum of $100,000 to qualify for these services; $1000 or $100 or even less, depending on the fund, will do. In the average fund, you will pay your adviser perhaps 1% of your investment every year, and the total cost of your having a mutual fund may be only 1.5% of your investment every year.

Mutual funds, in fact, have a populist tinge to them simply because they give average Americans the opportunity to prosper, to raise their own and their families' standard of living.

The Simplicity of Mutual Fund Investing. Investing in mutual funds is an easy matter.

You need not pay a stockbroker or financial planner up to 8.5% of your investment for guidance. You can do it on your

8

own, just by investing in no-load (no sales commission) mutual funds. Just write or telephone a mutual fund with an admirable track record, ask for a prospectus and application form, read the first and fill out the second, and send in your money. (But don't invest what is, for you, a large amount all at once. See Key 45, DOLLAR-COST AVERAGING.)

You may want to diversify even further by creating a portfolio of funds — some short-term bond funds and some intermediate-term, some high-grade and some high-yield, perhaps even some foreign-bond funds; some stock funds that invest in undervalued securities, some that invest in growing companies. You may want to keep investing in these funds, ideally by dollar-cost averaging. You must learn to follow a fund's performance, and calculate your profits or perhaps your losses. Of course, you also must decide when to sell any funds you own.

But to get started, phone for free mutual-fund literature.

Guides for the Perplexed. Once you have begun investing in mutual funds, or even before, you ought to read various periodicals. Good coverage of mutual funds is provided in such publications as *Barron's, The Wall Street Journal, Money, Kiplinger's Personal Finance Magazine, Business Week,* and *Forbes,* many of which have special quarterly or annual issues on mutual funds.

There are books, too, like *The Handbook for No-Load Fund Investors* (P.O. Box 283, Hastings-on-Hudson, N.Y. 10706; $45 — $115 in total, including monthly newsletter supplements); and the *Mutual Fund Sourcebook* (Morningstar, Inc., 53 West Jackson, Suite 460, Chicago 60604; $195 for a two-volume issue). The very serious mutual-fund investor should read *Mutual Fund Values,* published by Morningstar Inc. twice a month; $395 a year. These reference works are available in many libraries, as is the encyclopedic *Wiesenberger Investment Companies Service.*

For the industry point of view on funds: "Guide to Mutual Funds," published by the Investment Company Institute, 1600 M Street, N.W., Washington, D.C. 20036; phone

202-293-7700 ($5); "No-Load Mutual Funds: Investing the Easy Way," The Mutual Fund Educational Alliance Investor's Directory, 1900 Erie Street, Suite 120, Kansas City, Missouri 64116 ($5); and Directory, 100% No-Load Council, 1501 Broadway, Suite 312, New York, New York 10036 ($1).

The Mysteries of Mutual Funds. Everyone in the investment world is forever selling, besides all manner of securities, certitude. Stockbrokers, of course, say they know all the answers; so do academics; so do editors of mutual-fund newsletters; and so do the authors of mutual-fund books.

If the stock market has gone up, for example, we hear that investors are encouraged by the narrowing of the trade deficit or even an increase in unemployment; if the market goes down, it's due to profit-taking, or increasing interest rates, or other worries. (No commentator in history has ever talked about random fluctuations.) Then there is the vast store of conventional wisdom. Small-company stocks excel at the end of bull markets. The more diversified a fund is, the better. Never buy a fund that doesn't do exceptionally well in down markets. And so forth.

This book is an exception.

There are many burning questions that this book will not answer—though you may encounter occasional timid guesses.

Despite this disclaimer, the author does believe, among other things, that

• The past performance of a fund is not a perfect guide to its future performance, but it is your single best guide.

• A moderate form of market-timing is judicious.

• A fund should not be shunned simply because of its volatility—if the investor is fairly sophisticated and the fund has consistently rebounded.

• The stock market contains pockets of efficiency, not pockets of inefficiency; much of the time, stocks are too high-priced or too low-priced.

• The absence of gold and other precious metals from a portfolio will not be sorely missed.

• The stock market bobs up and down, but over the long run

it will bob further up than down.

• Over the short term, the stock market, as someone has said, will do whatever makes the largest number of people look foolish.

• Because conditions are forever changing, and human emotions are involved, the investment world will always be somewhat unpredictable. To quote the newsletter writer Cato Ohrn, "In the world of investing, water does not always boil at 212 degrees Fahrenheit."

• Finally, mutual funds are the solution for almost anyone searching for the best way to invest in almost anything whatsoever.

1

WHAT IS A MUTUAL FUND?

A mutual fund is a company that makes investments, usually in securities (stocks, bonds, and the like). If a mutual fund buys ten stocks and ten bonds, and you then buy shares of the fund, you will own a portion of those 20 securities — the amount depending on how much you invest.

The word *fund,* obviously, means a pool of assets. *Mutual* means that investors band together to buy securities.

The formal name for the most popular type of mutual fund is open-end investment company. The term *open-end* means that the company can always issue more shares; if investors flood a fund with new money, the fund can simply keep the money in cash (that is, money-market funds or Treasury bills), or buy more stocks, bonds, or whatever.

Mutual funds make a profit by charging fees to their shareholders. These fees, as we shall see, vary quite a bit from one fund to another.

The first mutual fund in this country was set up in Boston on March 21, 1924. Its net assets, $50,000, were fully invested in 45 stocks, including 50 shares of General Motors at 13¼. At the end of its first year, the fund had a mere 200 shareholders. Today that fund, Massachusetts Investors Trust, is one of the largest stock funds, with over $1 billion in assets and 85,000 shareholders.

Now there are over 3000 mutual funds — more than stocks on the New York Stock Exchange. But most people still keep their money in the bank. And most investors prefer money-market funds and fixed-income (bond) funds to stock funds.

Why People Buy Mutual Funds

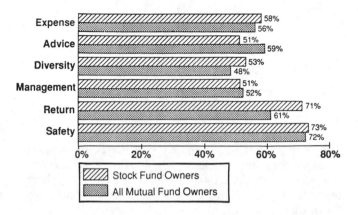

In fact, investors who gravitate toward mutual funds tend to be older — 50 or so. Perhaps older people have the money to invest; perhaps, over the years, they've learned the wisdom of buying mutual funds as opposed to buying individual stocks, bonds, and other securities on their own.

There seem to be two distinct types of shareholders: very sophisticated ones, and investors who know hardly anything at all. True, the subject of mutual funds can be confusing. It's a broad, somewhat complex field, the jargon is often imprecise, the rules and regulations abstruse. It takes a while to understand the difference between closed-end and open-end funds, no-loads and "pure" no-loads. But everyone can do it, and this book offers the keys to that understanding.

The different classifications of mutual funds often seem fuzzy at the borderlines. Reading mutual-fund prospectuses is about as much fun as reading the tax code. It's easy to confuse the names of funds — Merrill Lynch Phoenix with Phoenix; Neuberger and Berman Guardian with Guardian Park Avenue; the 26 different funds with the word American in their titles.

But if you learn a little at a time — even a few keys a day — you shouldn't feel overwhelmed.

2

THE BENEFITS
OF DIVERSIFICATION

If you had bought $10,000 worth of Walbro stock on April 1, 1987, a year later your holdings would have been worth $16,800 — a 68% gain.

If you had bought $10,000 worth of Digital Equipment on April 1, 1987, a year later your holdings would have shriveled to $6500 — a 35% loss.

Between these two extremes, you could have diversified — bought both stocks, for $5000 each, and emerged with $11,650, a profit of 16.5%.

Diversification, in fact, should be a goal in all your investing decisions. If you put all of your eggs in one basket, and drop that basket, your nest egg may wind up being scrambled.

Of course, if you knew of one stock whose price would inexorably rise year after year, there would be no reason for you to invest in anything else.

But there is probably no such stock. Even prosperous, well-run companies — IBM, Johnson & Johnson, Union Carbide — falter and stumble. They lose enormous lawsuits, like Texaco. Or their business suddenly turns sour, as IBM's

15

did in the early 1990s. Or tough competitors come along and steal away their business. Or their promising new product turns out to be a dud. Or indispensable company officers leave. Or the stock's price rises so high that, in response, many shareholders sell — and the price sinks below its reasonable value. Or business in general goes into a tailspin.

It's just as wise to diversify your holdings in bonds and other fixed-income investments. One reason: If you own only long-term bonds (those that will repay your investment in ten or more years) and interest rates rise, the value of your original investment will plummet. On the other hand, if you own only short-term bonds (due to be paid off in one to three years), the interest you receive may be rather anemic.

Granted, there's a rough relationship between risk and reward. The more diverse your portfolio, the less likely that you will be blessed with enormous profits. Generally, but not always. Proper diversification does not necessarily lead to mediocrity. Two of the very best-performing funds have been Fidelity Magellan and Vanguard Wellington. Yet both are about 90% as well diversified as the 500 stocks in the Standard & Poor's index.

But to afford a nicely diversified basketful of securities on your own, you must be fairly rich. To purchase a portfolio of 15 stocks, you would need around $30,000. Let's say that the average price of a stock is $20. You buy 100 shares of each. (It's cheaper to buy "round lots" — 100 shares or multiples of 100 — rather than "odd lots".) That costs $30,000 (15 × $20 × 100). Add in commissions, and the cost rises to $31,000.

Mutual funds provide an inexpensive, nearly effortless way you can buy 30 or 100 or 500 stocks — for only $1000, or maybe as little as 20 cents. (One family of funds, 20th Century, has no minimum; it has accepted a purchase of 20 cents.)

Mutual funds thus offer you a cheap and easy way to diversify your investments — whether they be stocks, bonds, precious metals, real estate, or short-term debt instruments.

That is why, for the beginning investor, for anyone not especially well-to-do, they are a blessing.

16

3

MANAGING YOUR PORTFOLIO

There are investors with $300,000 — and more — in their portfolios who have almost no idea what percentage of their holdings are in stocks, what percentage in bonds, what percentage in real estate, and so forth.

They don't have a diversified portfolio. They have a mess.

These people aren't dumb. They have no doubt earned good money in their careers. They're just not smart investors.

Smart investors usually know, roughly, how their assets are allocated — how much of their total portfolio is invested in stocks, bonds, cash or short-term securities, real estate, and precious metals. And why. And when to consider shifting their allocations.

Building Your Portfolio. Money you have invested (not just "saved" for emergencies) makes up your total portfolio. (Your "net worth" includes other things you own, like cars and furniture.)

Usually you won't have any money to invest until

(1) you have enough saved in a cash-reserve fund for

17

emergencies (if, for example, the IRS claims that you erred on your tax return, and you owe a lot more, plus penalties);

(2) you've paid for the insurance you may need (life, health, disability, homeowner's); and

(3) you have enough cash on hand to pay your current bills.

The word *portfolio* can mean both your overall investments as well as your individual investment sectors—your "subportfolios." Typically, a prosperous investor has subportfolios of stocks, bonds, real estate, cash, and so forth. Your total portfolio might also be divided into your "personal" portfolio and your retirement portfolio—your Individual Retirement Accounts, Keoghs, SEPs, 401(k)s, whatever. Most people invest their retirement portfolios more conservatively than their personal portfolios, one good reason being that you normally cannot tax-deduct losses if they're in your retirement portfolio.

Every member of your family might have a different total portfolio, depending on their ages and objectives. A woman in her 20s might think of stashing away a good percentage of her funds in stocks: She has the time to wait out market declines.

A man approaching retirement should typically be skewed toward income-producing investments, like bonds. At that age, most people don't have many years of a money-making career ahead of them.

The composition of your total portfolio depends on not only your age, but also on your "risk-tolerance." The less likely you are to panic and sell your stock holdings when the market has plunged, the more risk-tolerant you are. (To a large extent, your risk-tolerance thus depends upon your investing sophistication—with what equanimity you can accept the normal zigzags of the stock market.)

Your total portfolio also depends on your wealth. The more prosperous you are, the more you can afford to lose (temporarily, at least) and, thus, the more investment risk you can afford. And in the long run, the more profits you may be able to make.

Finally, your total portfolio may depend on the direction

18

you think the various investment markets are heading. With mutual funds you can move your money from stock funds to bond funds to short-term money-market funds to all kinds of other funds — even real estate.

Naturally, you must keep track of your subportfolios and your total portfolio — along with your spouse's (his or her portfolio may be different because of your different ages) and your children's.

It's a formidable job. Just keeping track of the 12 to 15 different stocks needed to diversify an equity portfolio can be enormously time-consuming.

The solution, once again, is mutual funds.

For your stock subportfolio, invest $3000 and you can own shares of hundreds of different stocks — small-company stocks and blue chips, risky stocks and safe stocks. (Vanguard's Index Trust-500 Series will provide you with a portfolio mimicking the composition of the Standard & Poor's 500.)

For your bond subportfolio, invest $2500 and you can own shares of 50 to 200 different bonds. (T. Rowe Price New Income will provide you with about 60.)

For real estate, invest $2500 and you will own shares of Fidelity Real Estate, which invests in a variety of real estate investment trusts and stocks.

For precious metals, invest $1000 and own shares of the Lexington Goldfund.

For a total expenditure of $9000 you can thus have a rounded total portfolio of stocks, bonds, real estate, and precious metals. (Spend more, and you can spread your net to include international stocks and international bonds.)

In short, mutual funds can readily provide you with manageable subportfolios and a manageable total portfolio.

Mutual funds can also provide you with a *managed* overall portfolio. Instead of your deciding how to allocate your assets, some funds will do everything. For openers, there are "balanced" funds, which invest in both stocks and bonds, leaning toward one or the other when their managers think the time is ripe.

4

INVESTMENT STRATEGIES

Your overall goal in making investments should be self-evident: to buy when prices are low and to sell when prices are high. (Or to buy average and sell high, or to buy high and sell still higher.) To reach that goal, you must follow a tested, logical strategy — or trust to luck.

Many different strategies can work.

Many mutual funds buy the stocks of companies whose earnings are rising: the "momentum" strategy. Value Line funds target stocks of companies whose earnings are rising, and whose stock prices are rising, too — lest no one else discover the stock for years, and its price goes nowhere. (There's a danger in being right too soon.)

Another tried-and-true investment strategy is to buy stocks that are underpriced: Bad news may have driven their prices down into the bargain basement. In any case, the assets of such companies, and their earnings, indicate that their prices should be significantly higher. This is the "basic value" approach, outlined in Benjamin Graham and David Dodd's classic investment book, *Securities Analysis*. Among the funds that attempt to follow this strategy are Mutual Shares,

Vanguard Windsor, Merrill Lynch Phoenix, and Gabelli Asset.

Unfortunately, undervalued securities can proceed to become drastically, horrendously, nightmarishly undervalued — and remain that way for years. Or a stock that seems undervalued may prove to warrant its low esteem. Batterymarch, a respected money manager that seeks out undervalued securities, is famous for having bought Braniff stock *a few hours* before the company declared bankruptcy. Many an ugly duckling, it is wise to remember, grows up to be an ugly duck.

The funds that have followed the simple strategy of buying and holding blue chip stocks, like IBM and GE, have done well enough. By sticking with companies that pay respectable dividends and that regularly raise those dividends, these funds have maintained good rates of total return.

Some funds buy a diversity of small-company stocks, trusting that the winners will eventually return far more than the losers. Diversification is the key here. While it's possible to lose 100% of an investment in a small company, it's also possible to make 1000% — or more.

Other funds keep shifting into various sectors of the economy — health care, automobiles, technology — that seem poised to prosper. Peter Lynch, who used to run Fidelity Magellan, followed this strategy.

All of these stock-picking strategies make sense — and can be more profitable than just buying a basketful of stocks.

Strategies for buying fixed-income investments, or precious metals, or real estate, may be different from the strategies for buying stocks. With bonds, for example, you may want to move from short-term to intermediate-term to long-term, depending on the way you think interest rates are heading. But whatever you invest in, you need a strategy — unless your intention is to trust to luck.

You could decide which strategy appeals to you, and follow it on your own. But staying with any investment strategy when it doesn't seem to be working anymore sometimes requires superhuman discipline. That's why you are generally better off investing in a mutual fund run by a professional portfolio manager who adheres to a particular strategy that you feel comfortable with. (A fund's prospectus will usually tell you its investment strategy.) And the keys that follow will help you decide on which funds are best for you.

Which strategy do the professionals prefer? Opinions vary. Samual Eisenstadt, director of research for the Value Line Investment Company, points out that the momentum strategy (which Value Line funds follow) tends to be profitable just at times when the "basic value" strategy is faltering, and vice versa. His suggestion: Buy at least two different funds, one of which seeks stocks with rising earnings, the other of which looks for undervalued stocks.

Whether or not you follow this specific advice is a personal decision. But the overall message — that diversification is important — should be followed by every investor in mutual funds.

5

WHY INVESTORS
NEED ADVISERS

Someone hired to manage your investments is called an investment adviser, money manager, or financial planner. In the case of a mutual fund, the person is called a portfolio manager.

Ideally, as explained in Key 4, a portfolio manager will follow a sensible investment strategy, whether it be looking for stocks from companies that are flourishing, or buying stocks that appear to be selling for 60 cents on the dollar.

A portfolio manager will probably also have access to information sources that may elude you. He or she may have analysts on staff or on call at brokerage houses—analysts who dine at fast-food restaurants before deciding whether the franchisor will prosper, or who contact a company's suppliers and competitors to check on its current prosperity and future prospects. A portfolio manager can also phone, or visit with, the chief executives of giant corporations, querying them about the state of their business and their plans for the future.

Besides the discipline to follow a sound investment philosophy and better access to current, important information, a skillful portfolio manager will be relatively immune to the psychological pitfalls that beset the amateur. Among them:

Averaging down. You buy a stock at, say, 20. It goes to 15. To prove to yourself (and to your stockbroker) that you weren't a complete idiot for buying it, you buy more. "It's even more of a bargain now," you tell yourself. True, buying more might be a good idea if you were *sure* of the reason for the stock's decline—and sure that it would rise again. (At Neuberger and Berman when a stock goes down significantly, portfolio managers must either sell—or demonstrate their confidence by buying more shares.)

Being reluctant to sell losers. Selling a stock that's in the dumps would be an admission of your having made an error. Many investors can't accept that. They hold on...and on. Whereas many professional investors automatically sell stocks that have declined 10–15% below their purchase price. Susan Byrne, who runs the Westwood Fund, likens a declining stock to a problem child, demanding too much attention. She'll dump it from her portfolio—unless she's so familiar with it that she knows its decline is only temporary. Michael Price, who runs the Mutual Series funds, sells losers because getting rid of them "clears my brain." And his ego isn't involved: "I make lots of mistakes," he says cheerfully.

Being reluctant to buy former holdings. Investors who are averse to selling a losing stock, and thus admitting a mistake, are also averse to selling a stock, then reconsidering, and buying it again. But Peter Lynch, formerly of Fidelity Magellan, would. He would sell a stock at 50, and buy it a few weeks later, when it had climbed to 55.

Falling in love with a stock. If a stock has made a good deal of money for you, naturally you're grateful. You may even think it's "unfair" for you to sell it. And it's all-too-human to want to keep the stock, even if it starts misbehaving. Patricia Bannan, the young portfolio manager of the Phoenix Balanced Fund, reports that she sold Digital Equipment in early 1988, as soon as its earnings didn't meet her expectations— although DEC had made her fund quite a bundle in the previous years. "It's still a great company," she says. "But don't confuse a company with its stock."

Succumbing to greed or fear. The most common error that

amateur investors make is buying high and selling low. It's a frightfully difficult temptation to resist. When stocks are rising, amateurs think that they will rise forever—and they must board the gravy train as soon as possible. So, greedily, they buy. When stocks are plunging, amateurs think that they'll sink into the pit—and sell in panic. That probably explains why, when anyone asks any group of ordinary investors how many have made money in the stock market, very few raise their hands.

Professional investors tend to be contrarians—to turn back when the crowd surges over the cliff. Even when the television set is set to MTV, they listen to a different drummer. On Oct. 19, 1987, when the Dow Jones Industrial Average fell 508 points, David Dreman—probably the most famous contrarian investment adviser—bought $25 million worth of stocks. But, in fact, almost any professional investor automatically thinks of buying when the market is dropping; when the market is soaring, the professional automatically thinks of selling. Says Irwin Lainoff, portfolio manager of the Neuberger and Berman Manhattan Fund, "When your stomach is churning, hold your nose and buy."

To sum up, what the managers of mutual funds have that distinguishes them from amateurs is the discipline to follow a sensible investment strategy; access to useful, up-to-date information; the courage to resist greed and fear; the bedrock self-esteem they need to readily admit their mistakes—and to think that occasionally they alone, among the throng of investors, may be right.

One more thing that professionals have that amateurs usually don't is time. Unlike the individual investor, investing isn't a hobby they practice in their spare moments. And unlike stockbrokers, investing isn't what portfolio managers do when they can take time out from selling.

Certainly amateurs can sometimes beat professionals. The race isn't always to the swift, the battle isn't always to the strong.

But as Damon Runyon observed, "That's the way to bet."

6

CLOSED-END FUNDS

In some cases, a *closed-end* or *publicly traded mutual fund* may be an even better choice for an investor than an *open-end* fund.

Shares of closed-end funds are bought and sold just like shares of stocks. Investors trade shares among themselves, just as do the shareholders of publicly held corporations, through a stock exchange or over-the-counter.

Other key differences between closed-end and open-end funds:

• The price per share of a closed-end fund doesn't necessarily match what the fund's portfolio is worth. The price depends on whatever the closed-end fund's shareholders are willing to accept for their shares. And, oddly enough, you often pay less for the shares of a closed-end fund than they are inherently worth.

• The portfolio manager of a closed-end fund doesn't see any investors' money coming in or going out: buyers buy from sellers. So the number of shares in a closed-end fund is fixed. With a mutual fund, the number of shares seesaws, depending on whether more investors are buying or selling.

• Because you buy or sell the shares of a closed-end investment company through a stock exchange or over-the-counter, you pay a commission to brokers who handle the transaction. With ordinary no-load mutual funds, you pay no commissions at all.

Closed-end funds have one nasty side to them. If you buy stock funds when they are first offered for sale, you will almost automatically lose money — because the fund's shares are offered at their actual value, then almost always start trading at a discount. Even funds launched by famous investment advisers, like Martin Zweig and Mario Gabelli, wind up selling at a discount. So: Don't buy a new closed-end fund that invests in stocks. (Closed-end bond funds are less likely to trade at a discount.)

Is the discount a plus or a minus? In general, a plus. True, you could buy shares of a closed-end at a sizable discount, then sell them a few years later at an even more sizable discount. But because of the discount, closed-end funds usually don't retreat so much in a declining market. Even better, some closed-ends eventually become open-end, or liquidate — usually at the instigation of their frustrated shareholders — and realize a profit when the discount is closed. This is what happened with the Japan Fund and with Emerging Medical Technology, both of which went open-end.

A closed-end fund enjoys another advantage: The portfolio manager need not keep any assets in cash to cover possible redemptions. Even if the market tumbles, the manager won't be forced to sell any sound securities to cover shareholders' panic selling. He or she is free to do what many experts think they should do in a declining market: Buy.

Mario Gabelli is unusual in that he manages both an open-end mutual fund (Gabelli Asset) and a closed-end fund (Gabelli Asset Trust). Which is better? He thinks a closed-end fund is preferable for long-term investors. But if you buy and sell fairly rapidly, he would recommend buying a no-sales-commission open-end fund — to avoid the commission costs of trading in and out of closed-end funds. Studies have shown that you can make money in closed-end funds simply by buying them when their discounts are unusually high.

The *Value Line Investment Survey* rates closed-end funds on both their timeliness and their financial soundness. You can consult *Value Line* in most large libraries.

The Wall Street Journal and other large newspapers list the net asset values of closed-end stock funds and their discounts on Mondays, the NAVs of closed-end bond funds and their discounts on Wednesdays.

Closed-Ends Versus Open-Ends

Type	How to buy shares	Sales price	Shares outstanding
Open-End	Directly from fund or through a salesperson	Net asset value	Varies
Closed-End	Stock exchange	Market price	Limited

7

TOTAL RETURN

Far and away the best way to evaluate any fund is to check its *total return*. Not the yield or regular income, not the distributions, not the appreciation in the fund's price per share.

What happened to your original investment in a mutual fund is your total return. A synonym: total profit or loss.

Total return includes everything — dividends, interest, capital gains, capital losses, even income from stock options (the fund may have sold investors covered calls — the right to buy stocks at a certain price). The total return is expressed as a percentage of the original net asset value — at the beginning of a week, month, quarter, year, or whatever. A total return of 20% for a year means that your investment increased by 20% during those 12 months. In this case a $1000 investment on January 2 would be worth $1200 at year-end on December 31 — if you reinvested all your distributions (realized gains, interest, dividends).

When you join a mutual fund, you have a choice. You can have all your distributions reinvested in new shares; you can reinvest just income, not capital gains; or you can have all distributions sent to you. And unless you reinvest all distributions, you won't own any more shares than you did originally (unless the fund splits its shares). Thus, if you did not ask to have your distributions reinvested, your total return may be different from the official total return. The official version assumes that you reinvested all your distributions. If you did not, your total return may be more, or less, than the official total return, depending on how the fund fared after the distribution.

To calculate a fund's total return over (say) a year, you must know not only (a) what the net asset value was at the start of the year and at the end of the year, and (b) the amount of interest and capital gains per share, but you must also know the net asset value at the time of the distribution—the price at which your dividends and capital gains were reinvested.

Most mutual-fund trackers assume that all distributions were reinvested, for the simple reason that this is what most investors do. But at least one monitoring service just adds the distributions to the overall pot. Usually the difference in the total returns isn't earth-shattering.

Here's the formula to figure out a fund's total return during the year if you reinvested your distributions:

(Yearend # of shares *times* yearend NAV) *minus*
(# of shares you owned at beginning of year *times*
beginning NAV) *times* 100 *divided by*
(beginning # of shares *times* beginning NAV)

An example: A fund's net asset value at the end of one year was 40. At the end of the next year the net asset value was 42. During the intervening months, the fund made distributions of $1.00 in dividends per share and $5.00 in capital gains. These distributions were invested when the net asset value was $41—which bought .146 shares (1.0 plus 5.0 divided by the net asset value, 41).

This works out as follows:

$(1.146 \times 42) - (1 \times 40) \times 100 / (1 \times 40) = 20.33\%$

The mutual-fund listings in most newspapers rarely provide a fund's total return over various time periods. For that, you should consult a newsletter, magazine, or one of the books mentioned in the Introduction.

8

EVALUATING FUND PERFORMANCE

It may seem obvious that, when you consider buying shares in any mutual fund, you should pay the most attention to its past performance, to its track record — to how profitable it has been.

Obvious it may be, but you may nonetheless get an argument. Many academicians insist that a fund's track record is useless as a guide. The prices of stocks, bonds, and other securities, these theorists claim, are almost always exactly what they should be, because they are based on the latest, best-available information. In a word, the market is "efficient."

The only reason that any fund does better or worse than average, the academicians are confident, is its level of risk. The more speculative the investment, the greater the chance of high profits or steep losses. Thus, a fund that has been doing well, as time goes by, will become a mere average performer. A fund with a bad record will eventually pull up its record to average. Funds have splendid records or poor records only because, statistically, a few funds will always outperform or underperform the averages — briefly.

It's true that most mutual funds will, over the years, become close to average performers. It's true that many funds that are top performers one year rarely repeat the next, and that many poor-performing funds tend to bounce back. But it's also true that the funds that generally do the best have portfolio managers who scrupulously follow a sound investment strategy. And the mere fact that the number of funds with above-average or below-average records is similar to the number one would expect, mathematically, is not proof that only chance is at work.

A more reasonable view is that securities prices — especially stock prices — are frequently too high or too low. After all, those prices depend on human psychology, which tends to overemphasize extrapolation from the present to the future and therefore may bid prices up too high or too low.

Many studies have shown that, over the years, a basket of stocks with low price-earnings ratios will outperform baskets with medium or high price-earnings ratios. In fact, the Value Line group has demonstrated that stocks chosen because their earnings have been growing will also outperform the market — and so will small-company stocks. Thus, it is possible to use rational criteria to select stocks that will outperform the market and to select mutual funds that will do better than their competitors.

Even granting that it's better to buy shares in a fund with good performance history rather than a mediocre or poor history, there's a sticky problem. What constitutes a good performance record?

Here is what 15 mutual-fund authorities* consider to be the key criteria in choosing funds, in descending order of importance:

A. The fund consistently has performed better than other similar funds. (A fund that invests in blue chips does better than other funds that also invest in blue chips.)

B. The fund has made enormous profits over the years — despite a few miserable years when the fund faltered.

C. The fund has consistently made a profit.

D. The fund consistently does better than the market indexes — like the Dow Jones Industrial Average.

These criteria aren't mutually exclusive, of course. A fund that regularly bests the competition (A) may have made enormous profits over the years (B), may have been a consistent winner (C), and may have done better than the market indexes (D). Indeed, in considering whether to purchase a fund, you should check all of these benchmarks.

Besides, the "right" answer depends on the individual investor. B is the better choice for the person who buys and holds, someone in for the long pull, who doesn't panic and sell out when the market has plunged. C may be the better choice for the very conservative investor, particularly someone older, or someone who needs income to live on.

As for which performance time-period to emphasize, when these same authorities were given a choice among four different performance rankings, they chose them in this order:

A. Best: Average 10-year record, excellent 3-year record.

B. Next best: Excellent 5-year record, mediocre 1-year record.

C. Third best: Average 5-year record, excellent 1-year record.

D. Last: Excellent 10-year record, average 3-year record.

In sum, a fund's 3-year and 5-year records seem the most vital. But do also pay attention to the 10-year and 1-year records. And take into consideration whether, during the period under study, the portfolio manager has changed.

---

*The panelists: Burton Berry, editor, "No-Load Fund X"; William F. Crawford, president, Investment Company Data; William E. Donoghue, author, *No-Load Mutual Fund Guide;* William G. Droms, professor of finance, Georgetown University; Norman G. Fosback, editor, "Mutual Fund Forecaster"; Patricia A. Ganley, former managing editor, "United Mutual Fund Selector"; Sheldon Jacobs, editor, *The Handbook for No-Load Fund Investors;* Kathleen Quigley Lantero, managing editor, Wiesenberger Investment Companies; Royal L. LeMier, editor, "Mutual Fund Specialist"; David H. Menashe, publisher, "Fundline"; Joe Mansueto, publisher, *Mutual Fund Sourcebook;* Paul A. Merriman, author, *Market-Timing With No-Load Mutual Funds;* Gerald W. Perritt, editor, "The Mutual Fund Letter"; Alan Pope, author, *Successful Investing in No-Load Funds;* Jay Schabacker, president, Schabacker Investment Management.

9

STOCK AND BOND INDEXES

Indexes are models of the stock or the bond markets as a whole. If you want to know how the "market" has been doing, and how your own portfolio has been faring in comparison, you would check a suitable index.

The Dow-Jones Industrial Average of 30 stocks is probably the best-known index. It's simple and it keeps pace with more sophisticated indexes. But it exaggerates market movements, and it includes only blue-chip stocks. It's also only an average: the stock of AT&T, with a market value of $64 billion, has the same weight as the stock of Bethlehem Steel, with a market value of $1 billion.

Standard & Poor's 500 Stock Index is the one used by most professional money managers. But it, too, is heavily slanted toward large companies, most of which are listed on the New York Stock Exchange. And because its holdings are market-value-weighted, the fortunes of a giant, widely held company like IBM can have a distorting influence. From time to time the components of the S&P change, as companies merge or fail. In all, the index represents about 80% of the market value of the NYSE stocks.

But both the Dow and the S&P give short shrift to small companies. For that coverage you must turn to an index like the Wilshire 5000 or the Value Line Average.

There are many other indexes, including the Dow utility and Dow transportation, the S&P health-care, and so forth. The components of these indexes change from time to time, as companies fail, merge, or otherwise no longer meet the criteria set by the index-makers.

While there are hundreds of bond indexes, the best-known are the Salomon Brothers Index, the Shearson Lehman Brothers Indices, the Merrill Lynch Indexes, and the Moody's Index. But bond indexes are even trickier to use, because bonds vary by their risk and their maturities. For comparison, you must seek out a bond index that reflects the risk and the term of your own fund's holdings. Or better yet, compare your bond fund's performance against that of a similar fund.

In rating a stock fund, you should certainly use as one touchstone the fund's record vis-à-vis the S&P 500. But remember that almost all funds operate under a handicap: They usually keep some of their assets in cash or cash equivalents, just to cover possible redemptions by share-holders. They also have operating expenses, such as for trading commissions. (You yourself couldn't buy the S&P 500 without paying commissions.) Vanguard Index Trust— 500 has underperformed the S&P 500 by tiny percentages in almost every year of its existence.

Finally, bear in mind that every index has a twin — a bigger and better version. The twin is the same index with dividends or interest reinvested. This is the index you should use for any comparisons.

Over the years, dividends have accounted for about 40% of the appreciation of the stocks in the S&P 500.

10

ALL-WEATHER FUNDS

It's possible to invest in stock funds without suffering the full stomach-turning volatility of the market. You can buy shares of funds that won't fall as far, or even won't fall at all, when the market itself tumbles. *All-weather funds,* they're called.

Unfortunately, the term "all weather" is quite broad. A fund may fare well in winter as well as summer — and still have as many ups and downs as a rollercoaster. A fund may be a reassuringly stable performer — and have a history of only mediocre total annual returns.

These funds may be "all weather," by the usual definition, but they may not be the best choices for investors seeking both stability and high returns.

Still, true all-weather funds exist. Certain mutual funds do nicely in bull markets and manage to acquit themselves with honor in bear markets. Beyond that, they remain stable and not volatile. And they enjoy superior track records.

One well-known example of a true all-weather fund is Vanguard Wellington, named after the Duke.

Wellington's total return in 1990 was minus 2.81%. (Total return: the growth or shrinkage of assets, combined with dividends and interest.) The market itself, as represented by the stocks in the Standard & Poor's 500 Index, was down 3.1% for the year. Fidelity Magellan, a classic fair-weather fund, lost 4.51%. Wellington's loss was its first since the early 1970s. If you had invested in the fund in 1980, over the next ten years your investment would have grown by an average of 14% a year. Yet Wellington bobs up and down only three-quarters as much as the S&P 500.

Another famous all-weather fund is Lindner. It gained 8.83% even in 1987, the year of the crash, and over the past ten years its average annualized return has been 16.5%. It bobs up and down 60% as much as the S&P 500.

Here are some reasons why certain funds may do well through thick and thin:

1. Like Wellington and Lindner, funds may buy under-valued securities — stocks and bonds of companies under a cloud. Such securities usually don't sink as much in declining markets because they're pretty far down in the dumps already. Generally, these stocks in such funds have low price-earnings ratios. (The p/e ratio indicates the amount that investors will pay for earnings, and thus is a measure of a stock's popularity.) In 1991 the typical p/e ratio of a stock was 17. The p/e ratio of a typical stock in the portfolio of the Lindner Fund was 12.

2. Funds may concentrate on stocks with high dividends. An example is Wellesley Income, which recently was yielding 8%. It concentrates on high-yielding stocks like utilities, but also searches for any that seem low-priced. When the market falls, stocks that pay decent dividends will not fall as much: The lower the price, the higher the yield — and the more attractive such stocks become. If a stock's price is $20, and it pays a $0.30 dividend per share every three months, its annual yield would be 6% ($1.20 divided by $20). If the price sank to $15 a share, the yield would climb to 8%.

3. Such funds may practice market-timing — selling their holdings when they suspect the market is beginning a major

decline, or has already entered one. An example is Mathers, which withdrew from the stock market before the 1987 crash. The fund gained an impressive 27.04% in 1987, and its average annualized return over the past ten years has been 11.87%. Mathers fluctuates only 23% as much as the S&P 500. Some funds practice market-timing indirectly, just by keeping more of their assets in cash when their managers can't find enough undervalued securities to buy.

4. Some funds diversify their holdings beyond just stocks. "Balanced" funds buy bonds as well, and such funds obviously are not generally as volatile as the stock market. A good example is Fidelity Balanced, which was up 1.95% in 1987 and gained 11.32% a year over the past three years. Other all-weather funds, called *asset-allocation funds,* diversify even beyond stocks and bonds. USAA Cornerstone, for example, splits its investments among five categories: foreign stocks, American stocks, gold, government securities, and real estate.

Perhaps the term "all weather" should be narrowed to mean a fund that doesn't do badly in market declines but also (a) has a superior record and (b) isn't especially volatile.

A simple way to identify volatile funds is to check their "betas." The beta coefficient is a number that measures stability. The S&P 500 is the standard—it has a beta of 1. A fund with a beta of 1.02 (like Fidelity Magellan) fluctuates 2% more than the S&P. On the other hand, a fund with a beta of 0.69 (Fidelity Puritan) is 31% less volatile. In looking for an all-weather fund, you might consider only those with betas lower than 0.80. Such funds would be 20% more stable than the market.

Below is an assortment of five funds with low betas and high returns. All of them are no-loads (no sales commissions), and investors can purchase shares directly from the funds.

Fund/Type	Return*	Phone	Beta**
Fidelity Balanced Balanced	11.32%	(800) 544-8888	0.47
Lindner Growth	8.96	(314) 727-5305	0.58
Mathers Growth	11.51	(800) 962-3863	0.23
Partners Growth	10.39	(800) 877-9700	0.80
Wellington Balanced	11.13	(800) 662-7447	0.76

*Average annual compounded return, 1987–1990
**Compared with 1, the volatility of the S&P 500.
Source: *Mutual Fund Sourcebook*

11

FAIR-WEATHER FUNDS

If all-weather funds perform well in both down and up markets, why would people buy any other kind of fund?

The answer is that all-weather funds don't always bless you with the highest profits. The single best-performing fund over the ten-year period 1980–1990 was Fidelity Magellan, with an annualized return of 21.27%.

Magellan is *not* an all-weather fund. It falls farther in bear markets than the market itself. It's 2% more volatile than the S&P 500; in 1987, its total return was not even 1%. Still, when the market goes up, Magellan soars to the heavens. It's a fair-weather fund, and—as its record suggests—that isn't necessarily bad.

In fact, many sophisticated investors prefer the more volatile fair-weather funds to all-weather funds. If you have the gumption to hold on to fair-weather funds during bear markets, or to buy them just as bull markets are getting under way, you usually will make more money than you would with all-weather funds. The best-performing funds over the same ten-year period, besides Magellan, include such volatile funds as AIM Weingarten (ten-year annualized return: 15%). Its beta is a lofty 1.12.

Funds that definitely aren't all-weather—like Magellan and Quasar—tend to remain fully invested in stocks, holding only a minimum of cash through thick and thin. They also tend to prefer small-company growth stocks, which are more volatile than blue chips.

Volatile funds tend to bounce back with renewed vigor after a market plunge. But there's no ironclad guarantee that volatile funds will bob up as well as down. A lurid example is 44 Wall Street, which has had a history of volatility. But a few years ago it bobbed down—and remained there. After making modest profits in 1982 and 1983, it lost 58.6% in 1984, 20% in 1985, 16% in 1986, 34% in 1987, and 19.6% in 1990.

Here is an assortment of fair-weather funds—those with high betas along with outstanding performance records:

Fund	Load	Return*	Beta	Phone
AIM Weingarten	5.5%	15.54%	1.12	(800) 347-1919
Columbia Special	None	14.12	1.32	(800) 547-1707
20th Century Vista	None	11.34	1.42	(800) 345-2021

*Five-year compounded annual return, to 5/31/91

12

FOUL-WEATHER FUNDS

Like all-weather funds, foul-weather funds tend not to sink very far in bear markets.

Foul-weather funds come in two main varieties: very conservative and very daring.

Conservative funds invest mainly in highly rated, safe securities, like utilities, which neither go up much in bull markets nor down much in bear markets, and blue chips. Beacon Hill, which hasn't had a losing year since 1974, invests in blue chips like Merck, IBM, and Procter & Gamble — and rarely sells any holdings. Another example of a conservative foul-weather fund is Valley Forge. While it, too, invests in conservative securities, it also market-times — buying blue chips when they seem clearly undervalued.

These conservative foul-weather funds do not fly very far in bull markets.

At the opposite pole are the daring foul-weather funds. These funds may sell short in declining markets. (Selling short means borrowing securities and selling them, hoping to buy them back later when their prices have declined.)

Probably the most noteworthy of such funds is Dreyfus Capital Value. A rather new fund, it does best when the market plummets. In 1987, Dreyfus Capital Value was up a spectacular 34.45%. A sister fund, Dreyfus Strategic Aggressive, which also sells short, was up 63.1%.

Are foul-weather funds suitable to your portfolio? You would probably be better off buying an index fund rather than an extremely conservative fund like Beacon Hill. The trouble with funds like Beacon Hill is that their performances tend to be only average. In 1987, Beacon Hill did about the same as the S&P 500, gaining 5.3%. Over the past ten years, its average annualized return has been only 10.7% — whereas the return of the Vanguard Index Trust-500, a replica of S&P 500 index itself, has been 13.47%. Besides, Vanguard's Index Trust-500 has only a little more volatility. Beacon's beta is 0.83, whereas the beta of Vanguard Index Trust-500 is 1.

On the other hand, Valley Forge's record is comparable to that of an index fund — and its beta is an astoundingly low 0.25.

Valley Forge would thus seem to belong in the portfolio of very conservative investors.

As for daring funds like Capital Value, they are obviously not suitable for investors who are averse to volatility. Capital Value can have enormous day-to-day volatility, even though it may never go down as much as the indexes. Still, daring foul-weather funds like Capital Value are also certainly worth considering for your portfolio, as ballast against fair-weather funds.

13

UNSEASONABLE FUNDS

Certain funds and families of funds perform miserably year after year.

Perhaps, as some academicians argue, it's just a tragic streak of bad luck, and such funds are no more likely to continue losing money than good funds are likely to continue doing well.

But it seems reasonable to believe that the portfolio managers of these unseasonable funds are just making amateurish investing mistakes, such as not diversifying, or buying high-fliers at exorbitant prices. While it would be enlightening to learn why these funds have fared so poorly, so consistently, the people behind them are not eager to talk to the press.

Certainly the Steadman Funds seem to be a cursed family, along the lines of the Jukeses. Herewith, members of the clan and their 10-year average annualized returns, along with that of an index fund:

Fund	1985–1990	1980–1990
Steadman American Industry	−12.18%	−8.38%
Steadman Associated	−4.28%	1.45%
Steadman Investment	−4.85%	−2.74%
Steadman Oceanographic	−15.16%	−11.68%
Vanguard Index Trust-500	12.78%	13.47%

Among individual funds with appalling long-term records: 44 Wall Street; Sherman Dean; American Investors Growth.

According to Michael Lipper, who monitors fund records, poor-performing funds are more likely to continue performing poorly than leading funds are likely to continue performing well.

Still, while unseasonable funds have lost a good deal of money for their shareholders, their year-in, year-out disappointing records serve a useful purpose: as evidence that a fund's track record can serve as a reliable harbinger of the future.

14

HIGH FEES AND OTHER HANDICAPS

Identifying funds with good performance records is the essential first step in deciding which to buy, but it isn't the only one. Even funds with good records may have handicaps, such as high sales charges and expenses. And if you are trying to decide between two funds, you should veer toward the one with fewer serious handicaps.

A handicap is a reason why a fund may not perform as well in the future as similar funds. For example, if a fund has a sales charge of 8.5%, you start off with only $915 out of every $1,000 of your money working for you, whereas with a no-load fund, you would have almost every penny working for you.

Here is how a panel of mutual-fund experts (see footnote, Key 8) evaluated the importance of various handicaps:

Serious

1. A fund has an 8.5% sales charge.

2. The fund's performance isn't matched by the risks it has taken. While it has been unusually profitable, it has also been unusually volatile. (See Key 22.)

3. The fund has a high "back-end load," or deferred-sales charge (which can be up to 6.5% if you redeem your shares within three to five years).

4. The fund has a high 12b-1 fee (1% or more per year) in effect. (See Key 17.)

Less Serious

5. The fund has a "medium load" — a 3% or 4% sales commission.

Least Serious

6. The fund is unusually large — with assets above $500 million. Giant size is more of a handicap for aggressive-growth or growth stock funds, not for stock income or fixed-income funds.

7. The fund's expense ratio (annual expenses divided by average net assets) is high — over 1.5%.

8. The fund has a redemption fee — typically, up to 1% for the first six months.

9. The fund buys and sells very frequently — its turnover is greater than 100%. (See Key 23.)

10. The fund's management fee is over 0.75% of average annual assets. (This is included in the expense ratio, so it may account for a high ratio.)

In choosing a fund, you should weigh its performance record against its handicaps. Better yet, find a similar fund with a similar performance record, and choose the one with fewer serious handicaps.

15

WHAT ARE LOADS?

A load is a sales charge you must pay to buy certain funds. You usually pay this commission to a stockbroker, financial planner, or insurance agent. About 60% of all funds (not including no-load money-market funds) carry front-end loads, those you pay when you first buy shares.

The highest sales charge permitted by the Securities and Exchange Commission is 8.5% of your original investment. (An exception: You may pay 9% for a fund, like Fidelity Destiny I or II, when you must contribute a large sum over 10 or 15 years.)

Over time, a full 8.5% sales charge can cost quite a bit of money. If you invest $10,000 in a fund with an 8.5% load, and the fund gains 10% every year, you'll wind up with $23,732.74 after ten years. If you had invested in a similar no-load fund (see Key 18), you would wind up with $25,937.42 after ten years — which is $2204 more. That's a difference of over 9%, not just 8.5%.

A load is usually a payment the fund makes to reward stockbrokers for selling you their funds. (With low- or medium-loads, the fund itself may keep the money.) Fortunately, stockbrokers generally seem to direct their clients toward the better-performing load funds. The load funds with the most net assets tend to be those with decent records, like Investment Company of America, Templeton World, Pioneer II, Affiliated, Merrill Lynch Retirement, and Washington Mutual.

A load fund has a few advantages over a no-load. Because loads tend to have more assets (brokers are selling them, after all), they also tend to have lower expenses—thanks to economies of scale. And if an investor is lucky, he or she may obtain good guidance from a stockbroker or financial planner.

But as a rule, sophisticated investors never buy full-load funds. Load funds do not perform any better than no-loads; in fact, during the early years an investor is in a fund, loads perform worse—owing entirely to the sales charge.

The argument has been made that load funds can buy better research, simply because they have more money. But the sales commission, in the case of a full-load fund, does not go to the fund but to its distributor and to salespeople.

The best argument against load funds is that you can virtually always find a similar no-load fund.

Load Fund	No-Load Double
Merrill Lynch Phoenix	*Mutual Shares*
Investment Company of America	*Windsor II*
PruBache High Yield	*Price High Yield*
Templeton World	*Price International*

Sophisticated investors may, nonetheless, occasionally consider "medium-load" funds, those that charge 3–6%, and "low-load" funds, those that charge 1–3%. (Funds that charge 6% to 8.5% are "full-load" funds.)

Some reasons these sophisticated investors give:

1. The fund is unique.

Example: Dreyfus Capital Value. But the argument can be made that new, unusual load funds will soon be imitated by new, unusual no-load funds.

2. The fund is new, and the portfolio manager has a glittering reputation.

Warren Buffett is a legendarily successful investor. If he were to open a load fund, buying shares might be irresistible.

3. The fund has a superior track record.

One investor had sworn that he would never invest in a load fund. Later he reported that he had purchased shares of Fidelity Magellan, which has a 3% load. Why? "I don't believe in fighting the tape, either," he explained. (Fighting the ticker tape means disregarding evidence — like the prices on a ticker tape.) Another load fund (3.75%) with an inimitable track record is SoGen International.

4. You invest an enormous sum of money.

The more you invest, the more the load shrinks. If you buy $100,000 worth of shares, for example, an 8.5% load might fall to 3%.

While 8.5% is usually the most you will pay for a full-load fund, you could wind up paying more. Around 40 funds also charge commissions when you reinvest distributions — dividends, interest, and capital gains. They invest your distributions at the offering price, not at a net asset value. Among these funds: the Franklin family. While the Franklin funds have good track records, you might be a little suspicious of any stockbroker or financial planner who pushes these funds. They have a special incentive.

Funds with 8.5% loads cannot levy commissions on reinvested distributions. Only funds with loads of 7.25% or less can charge commissions on reinvestments. If any fund charges exactly 7.25%, inquire further.

To determine whether a particular fund is a load or no-load, check the newspaper listings. All funds have a net asset value — what a share costs. But in the column where load funds show their higher "offering price," no-loads will carry the initials N.L. If a fund's net asset value and its offering price are the same, the fund has other charges instead of a front-end load, such as a deferred sales charge or a redemption fee.

To figure out what the sales charge of a fund is, subtract the net asset value from the offering price. If the first number is 13.47, and the second is 14.72, the difference is 1.25. Divide the difference (1.25) by the offering price (14.72), and you will obtain the sales charge: 8.5%.

16

REDEMPTION FEES

Some funds charge you a fee when you cash in some or all of your shares. Unlike a deferred sales charge or back-end load, redemption fees tend to be small, and they tend to vanish after a fairly short time.

Some no-load funds assess redemption fees, just to discourage investors who want to dart in and out. Lindner has a 2% redemption fee on shares redeemed within 60 days of purchase.

Whereas full front-end loads are certainly a serious handicap, a small redemption fee that disappears after two or three months is negligible. So don't turn away if you see an R next to a fund's name in newspaper listings.

17

12b-1 PLANS

The infamous 12b-1 ("distribution") plan was authorized by the Securities and Exchange Commission in 1980. Named after a section of the SEC's ruling, the 12b-1 plan was apparently intended to help funds — especially the no-loads — obtain more customers, by allowing them to use a percentage of their investors' assets to bring in new shareholders. Funds are permitted to use 12b-1 fees for marketing and distribution expenses — for advertising, sales literature, annual reports, and prospectuses, and to pay brokers who sell shares.

The fees are called "spread" fees by their advocates (they are spread out over the years) and "hidden" fees by their critics.

A case can be made for 12b-1 fees. Anthony Brown, portfolio manager of the Pax Fund, a fund that makes only ethical investments (see Key 34), says that the money enables him to advertise, make the fund larger, and thus shrink its expenses. Besides, if a 12b-1 fee is only 0.25% of yearly assets, as Pax's is, it's no great handicap. You would have to keep your shares of a fund with an 0.25% 12b-1 plan for 34 years to suffer the equivalent of an 8.5% load.

But critics point out that if the fee is 1.25% of net assets a year, after five years you have the equivalent of a 6.25% load, and after seven years, an 8.75% load.

Another problem is that financial planners and stockbrokers who sell 12b-1 funds obtain "trail fees" from the plans so long as their clients remain in those funds. Supposedly this is to keep the salespeople from eagerly pulling their clients out of the funds, perhaps to put them into new front-end load funds, just to obtain new commissions. But it's also a temptation for the salespeople to do nothing—to let their customers remain in funds that have turned into flea-bitten dogs.

Of course, in evaluating any fund, you should concentrate on performance. But if a fund has a high expense ratio (and 12b-1 fees contribute to the expenses), it's a distinct handicap. Most of the blue-chip funds—Vanguard, Neuberger and Berman, 20th Century Investors, Scudder—are "pure" no-loads. And the advisers of some other funds pay the cost of a 12b-1 plan out of their own pockets; still other funds have approved such plans, but have not put them into effect.

The SEC is considering a proposal to prohibit funds that have 12b-1 fees from calling themselves "no-loads."

18

NO-LOAD FUNDS

No-loads are not just ordinary mutual funds without sales charges. They seem to have different personalities as well. No-load people like to believe that they are doing society a service by allowing ordinary Americans to purchase securities cheaply, and thus share the wealth. People at no-loads are fiercely proud of their being no-loads.

James Stowers, president of the 20th Century Investors, a noted no-load family, says that his fund has no sales commission, and no minimum first investment, because he wants "to give everyone a chance."

But it's hard to make a case that no-load funds are more interested in the "little guy" than are loads.

While the impression may exist that no-loads have set lower minimum first investments, this doesn't seem to be the case—despite 20th Century Investors. Of the very largest funds, Vanguard Windsor (no-load) has a $3,000 minimum. Investment Company of America (5.75% load) has a $250 minimum; Affiliated (6.75% load), $250; Pioneer II (8.5% load), $50.

Besides, it was the no-loads that took the most advantage of the unpopular 12b-1 fees. Of course, it could be argued that no-loads needed them more. But it's unsettling that many of them eagerly instituted these "hidden loads," as they have been called.

As for individual funds, it is difficult to make a case that a family that charges full loads—like the American Funds out of Los Angeles or the Templeton funds—are somehow morally inferior to no-load funds, like the Steadman group. The American and the Templeton funds have superb performance records; the Steadman funds have appalling records. Besides, some families—like Fidelity—have no-load funds as well as load funds.

Still, the impression remains that the most admirable funds of all—for performance, for concern about their shareholders—seem to include a disproportionate number of no-loads or low-loads: Babson, Boston Company, Dreyfus, Evergreen, Fidelity, Financial Programs, Janus, Legg Mason, Neuberger and Berman, T. Rowe Price, Scudder, Strong, 20th Century, Value Line, Vanguard.

19

EXPENSE RATIOS

An efficient fund, a fund that's economical, will have lower expenses. Of course, the larger a fund, in general the lower its per-share expenses — because of economies of scale.

That's why the expense ratio takes into consideration a fund's size. A fund's expense ratio is calculated by dividing its annual expenses by its average net assets.

A fund's expenses include investment adviser's fees, legal and accounting fees, and 12b-1 fees, but not brokers' commissions, interest on loans, or income taxes.

An expense ratio over 1.5% is considered high, and 2% or more is regarded as excessive. Funds with high 12b-1 fees (over 0.25%), as you would expect, tend to have high ratios. (A study by Financial Planning Information in Cambridge, Mass., found that the expense ratios of funds with 12b-1 fees average about 45% higher than the expense ratios of funds without such fees.) Funds with management fees of 2% or more have high ratios, too. Fixed-income funds tend to have low ratios; specialized funds, high ratios.

Here are average expense ratios for the various categories of funds, as calculated by Financial Planning Information, using data from the Wiesenberger Investment Companies Service:

All funds: 1.15%	International: 1.35%
Aggressive growth: 1.18%	Metals: 1.32%
Low-term growth: 1.19%	Sector: 1.35%
Growth/income: 1.03%	Government: 1.02%
Balanced: 0.96%	Tax-exempts: 0.83%
Stock income: 1.20%	Technology: 1.27%
Income (flexible): 1.05%	Other: 1.51%
Income (senior securities): 1.01%	

Even though the expense ratio allows for the efficiencies of size, the fact remains that the larger a fund is, usually the lower is its expense ratio. Thus, as a fund grows larger, its expense ratio tends to shrink.

Poor-performing funds tend to have high expense ratios: Their net assets keep going down as shareholders bail out.

The argument has been made that if a fund has a consistently high expense ratio, its prognosis is poor: Eventually its performance will suffer. But this may be a case of putting the cart before the horse. If a fund does badly, shareholders exit — and the expense ratio climbs.

A high expense ratio can be a minor blemish on an otherwise top-performing fund. But again, in comparing similar funds, you should consider their expense ratios. Of course, there may be counterbalancing factors: A fund that allows a very low initial investment will have a relatively high expense ratio because it costs more to deal with a large number of small investors than a smaller number of large investors.

20

BETA: A MEASURE OF VOLATILITY

The term *beta coefficient* sounds forbiddingly abstruse, but it's a simple idea, and very useful.

The beta is a number that compares the volatility of a stock, or a stock mutual fund, with the volatility of the stock market in general as measured by the Standard & Poor's 500. The usual time frame is three years.

The S&P 500 index has a beta of 1. (Money-market funds have a beta of 0 — supposedly they carry no risk of any loss of principal through market fluctuations.) A security that goes up and down 20% less than the S&P 500 gets a beta of 0.80. A stock or mutual fund that fluctuates 15% more than the S&P 500 is assigned a beta of 1.15.

While a stock fund's beta is based on what has happened, it suggests what may happen, too — how far you can expect a fund to fall when the market falls, how far you can expect it to climb when the market climbs. The beta isn't a totally reliable guide, though. Funds with high betas sometimes do poorly in a bull market, and funds with low betas sometimes do even worse than average in bear markets. But most funds with low betas emerged from the October 1987 bloodbath healthier than those with high betas.

A stock may have a high beta because there aren't many shares outstanding—it's "thinly traded." So its price swings may be wide. Thinly traded stocks also tend to be small-company stocks, and another reason that they're volatile is that little is known about them. Fresh information, or rumors, can drive their prices way up or down. Besides, the prosperity of such stocks is obviously more susceptible to sudden changes of fortune.

The price movements of international stocks and stock funds do not correlate with the S&P 500, so their betas are not meaningful. The same applies to gold and precious-metals stocks and mutual funds.

Before buying any stock fund, find out what its beta is. (Various newsletters report on the betas of the leading funds.) You may not want to reject a volatile fund out of hand, but you should know whether the fund you are buying is all-weather or fair-weather. That way, you will probably know what to expect.

21

EVALUATING RISK

Obviously, "risk" means your chances of losing money on an investment. The worst risk is losing a big chunk of your principal, or all of it.

Risk would seem to be a treacherously difficult concept to measure, but that hasn't stopped certain academicians. To them, *risk* equals *volatility*. Certainly risk and volatility are at least cousins. Volatile stocks tend to be those of small companies with relatively few shareholders, little fish in shark-infested waters, forever facing danger—from the economy, from rivals, from customers.

One way that funds are penalized for their volatility is measuring their performance against their betas. A fund with a beta of 1.2 is expected to perform 20% better than the Standard & Poor's 500 Stock Index. If not...demerits.

Funds may also be penalized for having an unusually high standard deviation—how much the fund's monthly returns swing up and down. The standard deviation measures pure volatility, not volatility in relation to the S&P 500. For example, two funds may have a total return of 18% over 36 months. Fund A may have appreciated 0.5% every month; Fund B may have had big monthly swings, down 6%, up 30%, and so forth, but both in the end gaining 18%. Fund B's standard deviation figure would be higher.

One obvious objection to using the standard deviation as a measure of risk is that stocks and stock mutual funds shouldn't be faulted when they fluctuate upwards. Bobbing down is certainly bad, but bobbing up is kind of nice.

One mutual-fund monitoring service, Morningstar, has taken care of that objection. When it calculates a fund's risk-adjusted return, it doesn't give a fund black marks for those months when it provides a better return than you could have received from a totally risk-free investment — three-month Treasury bills.

Morningstar adjusts a stock fund's performance for risk by the following means: Take a fund's total return for each month. Subtract the return from that of a three-month Treasury bill. Add up all the months when T-bills did better than the fund. Divide by the number of months in the rating period (usually 36 months).

Yet, as we shall see, even Morningstar's unusually enlightened risk-adjusted ratings seem to be severe on many fair-weather funds.

Some other objections to the risk-volatility equation:

1. The beta coefficient is measuring human judgment — how warm, or how cool, investors have been toward particular investments. It seems inherently doubtful that the beta can be perfectly reliable when human beings aren't.

Besides, a low beta in a fund may conceal all manner of volatility — a stock that soars, a stock that sinks. Even one stock's beta may be misleading: "An admittedly exaggerated example," writes Arthur Williams III in *Managing Your Investment Manager* (Dow-Jones-Irwin, 1986), "might be a situation in which the president of a mining company absconded with $10 million in assets at the same time that a new mine worth $10 million to the company was discovered."

Indeed, a study in the *Financial Analysts' Journal* (March/April 1988) checked how three measures of risk supported the notion that the more risk a stock carries, the greater is its return. Beta proved an unreliable guide; the standard deviation was quite good. Best of all was the Value Line ranking of a stock for safety, which is derived from a blend of both a stock's standard deviation and its fundamentals — its balance sheet and income stream.

2. For years, high-yield ("junk") bond funds fluctuated about the same as high-grade bond funds, yet the former were far more risky — which is why their yields are so much higher. In a severe recession, the extra risk in high-yield bonds just might prove itself as many businesses go under.

3. You measure volatility by comparing how much a stock or a fund's price changes deviate from the S&P 500 — the beta coefficient. But you are thus comparing a stock or stock fund with a group of stocks from enormous, prosperous companies. (The use of the S&P 500 seems to stack the deck in favor of stocks and funds that emphasize blue chips.) Perhaps the volatility and the total returns from stocks and funds that invest in small- and medium-sized companies should be weighed against a more suitable index, like the Wilshire 4500 (Wilshire 5000 minus S&P 500).

4. From 1983 to 1991, small-company stocks did poorly — and so, of course, did many funds that invest in small-company stocks. Yet, over the years, small company stocks have performed better than large-company stocks. Why emphasize three- or five-year betas during a time that seems to have been an historical oddity? Besides, in 1991, small-company stocks began a significant recovery.

5. Clearly, a fair-weather stock fund should get credit for having demonstrated its elasticity — if it has a long, reliable record of climbing in bull markets despite its sinking in bear markets. Fidelity Magellan has such a record; should it receive the same treatment as a new fund that simply dropped in October 1987? A fair-weather fund with demonstrated elasticity might get even more credit if it has the same portfolio manager who guided it through feast and famine in the past. After all, no intelligent person doubted that Peter Lynch's Fidelity Magellan, after being caught in the crash of 1987, would rise again.

22

ALPHA: A MEASURE
OF RISK VS. REWARD

If the degree of risk you take matches the reward you can expect (not always true), and if a fund's beta is identical with its riskiness (it isn't), then you should be able to rate a fund manager's performance unerringly. You simply check the fund's performance against its beta. The lower the beta, and the higher the fund's performance, the better. Ideal would be a low beta and a high performance. But a high beta and a stratospheric performance would do as well.

The relationship between a fund's beta and its performance is called *alpha*. The higher the alpha coefficient, the better, but any alpha over 0 is desirable. An alpha of 0 indicates merely that the fund did as well as expected, given its volatility.

Here's how the alpha is calculated:

Let's say that, over the course of a year, risk-free Treasurys returned 8%. The S&P 500 returned 10%. Your fund returned 12%. Your fund's beta is 1.2 — 20% more volatile than the S&P 500.

You would expect your fund to return at least 8% — which is what Treasurys would have given you. But during the period under study, stocks returned 2% more than Treasurys. So you would expect your fund to return 8%, plus its beta (1.2) times 2%, the extra return of stocks. Or 10.4%. But your fund has actually returned 12% — 1.6% more than you could have expected. Its alpha is thus 1.6.

If your fund had actually returned 10.4%, its alpha would have been 0. Average. If it had returned 8%, its alpha would have been −2.4%.

The obvious question is: Do the best funds have positive alphas?

Here are some of the top-performing funds and their recent three-year alphas:

Acorn	−4.24
Fidelity Magellan	1.99
Lindner	−2.13
Neuberger and Berman Partners	−2.22
Wellesley Income	1.78

Next, here are five bottom-of-the-barrel funds and their alphas:

Afuture	−9.29
44 Wall Street	−10.5
Monitrend Value	−8.06
Sherman Dean	−10.5
Steadman Oceanographic	−28.8

Obviously, some of the very best-performing funds (Fidelity Magellan, Wellesley Income) have high alphas, and all of the worst-performing funds have low alphas. But several funds with good records—Acorn, Lindner, Neuberger and Berman Partners—have been punished too severely for their volatility.

In short, don't be beguiled by all the fancy statistics and the two decimal places. A fund's alpha is a useful but somewhat crude guide to its performance.

23

THE DANGERS
OF A HIGH TURNOVER

A fund that buys and sells securities quickly will have a high turnover—the rate at which it changes its holdings. A 100% turnover suggests that a fund has replaced its entire portfolio in a year.

Here's how a fund's turnover is calculated:

Take the value of purchases or sales during the fund's fiscal year—whichever is lower. (If you took both, you might be doubling the rate of trading.) Exclude fixed-income investments with maturities of a year or less. (Including them would be a little unfair: They would have been out of the portfolio in a short time anyway.)

Divide the dollar value of the securities bought, or sold, by the fund's average monthly assets during the year.

Multiply the result by 100, to express it as a percentage.

If a fund never sold or bought a single security during the year, its turnover would be 0%—0 divided by any figure whatever.

If a fund bought or sold $100 million worth of securities during the year, and its average monthly assets during the year were $100 million, its turnover ratio would be 100% (1×100). That implies a complete portfolio change during the year. Of course, the fund could just have sold 10% of its average holdings ten times a year.

A high turnover—over 100%—is certainly a smudge against a fund (see Key 14). It means that the fund has high commission costs; it also may mean that shareholders have high capital gains and high taxes to pay come April 15, if the fund has been selling winners. (Many smaller funds try to play off sales of stocks with big gains against sales of stocks with losses.) If a fund has a low turnover, it is holding onto its winners—and enabling shareholders to defer paying taxes on the fund's capital gains. (You do not pay capital-gains taxes on profits a fund has made until the fund sells those securities or you sell your fund shares.)

Some funds will have high turnovers one year, low turnovers the next. But some funds always seem to have high turnovers, and the question is whether the fund's total return compensates for the high turnover.

Thus, a fund that follows the momentum strategy—buying stocks that have been making money hand over fist—will usually have a high turnover. It will buy and sell as the market leaders change.

A fund that moves from industry to industry, following the economic climate, will also have a high turnover. A prime example is Fidelty Magellan. While its turnover in 1987 was a relatively low 96%, usually it's over 100%. In 1980, it was 338%.

Finally, poor-performing funds also tend to have high turnovers. Perhaps the high turnover is contributing to its poor record, but more likely the portfolio manager is frantically switching from stock to stock.

True, the cost of a high turnover will be reflected in the fund's total return. And the high turnovers of Dreyfus Strategic World (556% in 1990) and Fidelity Magellan aren't bothersome when you look at their consistently outstanding performances. But a high turnover will also affect the taxes you pay, and normally you would prefer to pay taxes later rather than sooner.

24

CLASSIFICATIONS OF MUTUAL FUNDS

The broad categories of mutual funds—stocks, bonds, short-term debt instruments—are too broad. Within each of these categories are many funds that are quite different from one another, and it's important to know the distinctions.

One reason is so you know what you're buying. There's a world of difference between a stock fund that sells short, trades options, and concentrates on small companies and another fund that simply invests in the bluest of blue chips, like IBM, General Motors, and Johnson & Johnson. The first, obviously, is far more risky. There's also a world of difference between a short-term bond fund and a long-term bond fund.

A second reason to be aware of the distinctions is so that you can compare the performances of various funds. If you want to know how well a fund like Acorn has performed, compare it with, say, Evergreen, which also invests in small-company stocks. Over ten years, the average annualized return of Acorn was 13.52%; of Evergreen, 13.09%.

Don't compare Acorn with, say, Valley Forge, which is in reality a money-market fund that occasionally buys a few blue-chip stocks selling at bargain prices. Valley Forge's ten-year averaged annualized return is only 9.97%. But with Valley Forge, you're getting far less volatility.

Classifying funds is tricky. A fund's prospectus may suggest one way of investing, one objective, but in real life it may invest differently. Or a fund may change its technique. A fund that ostensibly invests in small companies may veer toward larger stocks—with less potential for fast capital appreciation—as the fund grows larger. Or the investment climate may persuade a fund to alter its objective—for example, holding a lot of cash at a time when stocks seem overvalued.

Then too, like most demarcation lines, the lines between the various classifications can be fuzzy. If a fund owns small-company stocks as well as blue chips, is it "aggressive growth" or just "growth"? If its portfolio is about half high-dividend stocks and half bonds, is it a stock income fund or a bond income fund?

Making everything even more tricky is that there are no "official" classifications of funds that all rating services follow. One monitoring service, Lipper Analytical, doesn't call any funds "total return." ("People didn't seem to understand what they were," says Michael Lipper). And it labels the riskiest funds as "maximum capital appreciation," whereas "aggressive growth" is the usual term.

Not surprisingly, the various monitoring services may also classify funds differently. One service may decide that Freedom Gold & Government, which invests in a changing mix of gold stocks and government securities, is a gold fund; another may put it in the government securities category. Of course, where it's placed determines whether its performance is considered good or bad.

The closest thing to an official classification is the one issued by the Investment Company Institute (ICI), the trade association for mutual funds. Its classifications are regularly refined and expanded. Following is its list of 22 types of funds and their definitions. (The listing generally proceeds from stock to fixed-income funds.)

Most mutual-fund investors, by the way, are conservative. Recently 46.6% of assets in all mutual funds were in money market and short-term municipal bond funds; 30.4% was in bond and income funds; and 23% was in stock funds.

1. *Flexible portfolio funds* "may be 100% invested in stocks *or* bonds *or* money market instruments, depending on market conditions." This is the newest category: Other names for such funds are asset-allocation funds and total-return funds. These funds are actually more complex versions of balanced funds. Examples: Blanchard Strategic Growth, Rightime, Strong Total.

2. *Aggressive growth funds* "seek maximum capital gains.... Current income is not a significant factor. Some may invest in stocks of businesses that are somewhat out of the mainstream, such as fledgling companies, new industries, companies fallen on hard times, or industries temporarily out of favor. Some may also use specialized investment techniques such as option writing or short-term trading." Other "specialized investment techniques," we might add, can include selling stocks, index futures, and options short. Examples: Evergreen, Fidelity Magellan, Merrill Lynch Phoenix, Oppenheimer Time, Quasar Associates, Quest for Value, Strong Opportunity, Tudor, 20th Century Vista, Value Line Leveraged Growth, Weingarten Equity.

3. *Growth funds* "invest in the common stock of well-established companies. Their primary aim is to produce an increase in the value of their investments (capital gains) rather than a flow of dividends...." Examples: Fidelity Destiny I, Gabelli Asset, Growth Fund of America, Ivy, Janus, Legg Mason Value Trust, Neuberger and Berman Manhattan, Partners, Pennsylvania Mutual, T. Rowe Price New Era, 20th Century Growth.

4. *Growth and income funds* "Invest mainly in the common stock of companies that have had increasing share value but also a solid record of paying dividends. This type of fund attempts to combine long-term capital growth with a steady stream of income." Examples: Dodge & Cox Stock, Evergreen

Total, Guardian Mutual, Investment Company of America, Mutual Shares, Pioneer, Strong Investment, 20th Century Select, Vanguard Index Trust, Windsor II.

5. *Income (equity) funds* "seek a high level of current income... by investing primarily in equity securities of companies with good dividend-paying records." Examples: Decatur, T. Rowe Price Equity Income.

6. *Precious metals/gold funds* "maintain two-thirds of their portfolios invested in securities associated with gold, silver, and other precious metals." Some can actually buy bullion.

7. *Global equity funds* "invest in securities traded worldwide, including the U.S. ...."

8. *International funds* "invest in equity securities of companies located outside the U.S. Two-thirds of their portfolios must be so invested at all times to be categorized here." Example: Fidelity Overseas.

9. *Balanced funds* "generally have a three-part investment objective: (1) to conserve the investors' initial principal, (2) to pay current income, and (3) to promote long-term growth of both this principal and income. Balanced funds have a portfolio mix of bonds, preferred stocks, and common stocks." Examples: Fidelity Puritan, Phoenix Balanced, Wellington.

10. *Income (mixed) funds* "invest in income-producing securities, including both equities and debt instruments." The difference between this category and balance funds is subtle.

11. *U.S. Government income funds* "invest in a variety of government securities. These include U.S. Treasury bonds, federally guaranteed mortgage-backed securities, and other government notes."

12. *Ginnie Mae funds* "invest in mortgage securities backed by the Government National Mortgage Association. To qualify for this category, the majority of the portfolio must always be invested in mortgage-backed securities."

13. *Corporate bond funds* "buy bonds of corporations for the majority of the fund's portfolio. The rest of the portfolio

may be in U.S. Treasury bonds or bonds issued by a federal agency." Here, useful subcategories would be short-term, medium-term, and long-term corporate bonds.

14. *High-yield bond funds* "maintain at least two-thirds of their portfolios in lower-rated corporate bonds (Baa or lower by Moody's rating service and BBB or lower by Standard & Poor's rating service). In return for a generally higher yield, investors must bear a greater degree of risk than for higher-rated bonds." The more common name for these bonds, of course, is junk bonds. As in 13, categorizing such funds by their maturities would be useful.

15. *Global bond funds* "invest in the debt securities of companies and countries worldwide, including the U.S." Example: Scudder Global.

16. *Income (bond) funds* "invest at all times in a mix of corporate and government bonds."

17. *Long-term municipal bond funds* "invest in bonds issued by states and municipalities to finance...public projects. In most cases, income earned on these securities is not taxed by the federal government...."

18. *Short-term municipal bond funds* "invest in municipal securities with relatively short maturities. These are also known as tax-exempt money market funds."

19. *State municipal bond—long-term funds* "work just like other long-term municipal bond funds except their portfolios contain the issues of only one state. The advantage for a resident of that state is that income is free of both federal and state tax."

20. *State municipal bond—short-term funds* "work just like other short-term municipal bond funds except their portfolios contain the issues of only one state. The advantage for a resident of that state is that income is free of both federal and state tax."

21. *Money-market funds* "invest in...short-term securities.... These are generally the safest, most stable securities available, including Treasury bills, certificates of deposit of large banks, and commercial paper (the short-term IOUs of large U.S. corporations)."

22. *Option/income funds* invest "primarily in dividend-paying common stocks on which call options are traded on national securities exchanges. Current return generally consists of dividends, premiums from writing options, net short-term gains from sales of portfolio securities on exercises of options or otherwise, and profits from closing purchase transactions."

Missing from the ICI's classifications are "sector" or "specialty" funds—those that invest exclusively in, say, broadcasting companies or real estate. The ICI generally places all of them under "aggressive growth." This is probably a good idea, because it doesn't make much sense to compare the vast variety of sector funds against one another. (The ICI places public-utility funds under "growth and income," and—obviously—has a separate category for gold and precious metals.)

If you're not sure how a particular fund should be classified, despite its prospectus and its classification by the various monitoring services, check the fund's volatility. Funds in the same class tend to share similar betas. Aggressive-growth funds, for example, tend to be far more volatile than growth-and-income funds.

25

EQUITY FUNDS

"Equities" are investments where you own a piece of the action—like common stocks. They're the opposite of money you merely lend—bonds, Treasury notes and bills, Ginnie Maes, certificates of deposit. Mutual funds that invest mostly in stocks are usually called equity funds, not stock funds, because they may own convertible bonds as well, which can be exchanged for stock at a specified price.

Most investors in mutual funds prefer money-market funds and fixed-income funds to stock funds. Stocks scare many investors, especially since the crash of 1987. Perhaps it's because of their volatility. Perhaps it's because it's so easy to lose money in the market. Investors get a tip on a hot stock; they follow it for a while in the newspapers; it keeps going up; finally, they buy. Naturally, they are among the very last people to be interested in buying; now the stock doesn't just sink, but goes to hell in a handbasket.

Supposedly 90% of all stock-market investors wind up losing money.

But in exchange for the volatility of stocks, you can reap unusually high rewards—if you buy low and sell high, or just higher. The chart on the next page shows how stocks have fared, over the years, during various economic climates—deflation, price stability, disinflation and moderate inflation,

73

and rapid inflation. Compare the performance of stocks against the inflation rate (as represented by the Consumer Price Index), against bonds, against short-term obligations like Treasury bills and commercial paper, against housing, farmland, gold, and silver.

Only in periods of deflation have bonds exceeded the return on stocks; only in periods of rapid inflation have hard assets like real estate and precious metals matched or beaten the return on stocks.

In fact, putting everything together, stocks have been the single best-performing investment over the years—better than bonds, better than cash, better than real estate, better than precious metals. "Over the long run," write Roger G. Ibbotson and Gary P. Brinson in *Investment Markets: Gaining the Performance Advantage* (McGraw Hill, 1987), "U.S. stocks have topped the charts as the asset with the highest returns. One dollar invested in 1789 would have earned over an 8% annual return, and the money would have doubled roughly every nine years. Through the magic of compounding, investors would have made almost 5 million times their money in such equities."

During the 65-year period between 1926 and 1990, the Standard & Poor's 500 Index (including dividends) has appreciated during 45 years and lost ground during 20 years. In other words, if you had held a diversified basketful of stocks, over the course of any one year, your chances of making money were over 69%.

If you had held a basketful of stocks for any five-year period during those 65 years, you would have made money over 89% of the time; for 10 years, 98% of the time; and for 15 years or longer, 100% of the time—you would never have lost money.

Lessons: Stay in the market. Don't plunge into the market in any particular year: If you had invested in stocks at the beginning of 1929, you might not have shown a gain until 1943—15 years later. Finally, own a diversified portfolio of stocks, one that should do at least as well as the S&P 500.

ANNUAL RATES OF RETURN UNDER VARIOUS ECONOMIC CONDITIONS

	CPI**	Stocks	Bonds	T-Bills†	Housing	Farmland	Gold	Silver
Deflation								
1871–1896	-1.5%	5.5%	6.4%	5.4%	N/AV	N/AV	*	-6.8%
1892–1895	-3.3	-2.5	5.1	4.1	1.5%	N/AV	*	-8.0
1919–1922	-2.0	5.0	4.2	6.7	1.0	-12.1%	*	-18.2
1929–1932	-6.4	-21.2	5.0	3.0	-3.9	-12.3	*	-19.8
Average	-3.3	-3.3	5.2	4.8	-0.4	-12.2		-13.2
Price Stability								
1896–1900	0.3	26.1	3.3	3.3	0.0	9.3	*	-1.0
1921–1929	-1.3	20.2	6.4	5.4	4.4	-2.8	*	-3.3
1934–1940	1.0	12.2	6.2	0.7	7.2	3.9	6.3%	1.0
1952–1955	0.3	24.5	3.5	1.5	4.5	6.5	*	2.1
Average	0.1	20.8	4.9	2.7	4.0	4.2		-0.3
Disinflation & Moderate Inflation								
1885–1892	0.0	4.5	4.4	5.1	N/AV	N/AV	*	-4.5
1899–1915	1.3	8.2	4.1	5.3	5.7	N/AV	*	-0.5
1942–1945	2.5	26.1	4.5	0.9	10.0	18.1	*	-3.3
1951–1965	1.6	16.5	2.2	3.5	5.5	6.7	*	3.0
Average	1.4	13.8	3.8	3.7	5.3	6.2		-1.3
1981–1985	3.8	20.2	22.0	9.6	5.3	-8.1	-0.5	-16.4
Rapid Inflation								
1914–1919	13.3	11.6	2.1	4.7	17.5	14.7	*	15.5
1940–1947	6.8	12.3	2.6	1.0	12.2	18.5	*	8.6
1949–1951	5.8	24.8	0.9	2.3	10.2	21.7	*	20.5
1965–1971	4.0	6.4	6.1	6.8	10.3	12.7	31.6	23.7
1971–1981	8.3	5.8	3.8	8.8	10.3	14.6	28.0	21.5
Average	8.3	12.2	3.1	4.7	12.1	16.4	11.9	18.0

*Under government regulation, the U.S. market price of gold did not change during this period.
**Consumer Price Index
†U.S. T-Bills and Commercial Paper
Averages do not double count overlaps. N/AV = Not Available
Source: Morgan Stanley Research

26

SPECIALTY/SECTOR FUNDS

These are a hybrid between individual stocks and typical mutual funds. They are more diversified than the former, less diversified than the latter. They are variously called specialty funds, single-industry funds, and sector funds, but what they do is concentrate their investments in a rather narrow area.

Not considered specialty or sector funds are those that invest only in small-company stocks, or in "socially responsible" companies, or in a variety of investments that mirror an index, or in the securities of only one foreign country.

As for funds with a narrower focus, perhaps they should be segregated according to the amount of their diversification, with the broader ones being called specialty funds and the concentrated ones, sector funds. Specialty funds seem able to offer almost the diversification of normal mutual funds. Among the specialty funds are those that invest in a variety of real estate (real estate investment trusts and real-estate stocks) or in the stocks of companies in one region of the United States.

Among the sector funds are those that invest in just agriculture, chemicals, health care, precious metals, insurance companies, technology, brokerage firms, or the entertainment industry. Fidelity Investments pioneered in offering a whole panoply of sector funds in 1981, and the family now offers 36 different sector funds, from energy to utilities. Financial Programs and Vanguard also now offer a series of sector funds.

For most investors, sector funds — as opposed to specialty funds — should probably be off-limits. Such funds tend to be extemely volatile, simply because they don't have the diversification of normal mutual funds. (While funds that invest in utilities seem to qualify as sector funds, they probably should be considered specialty funds, simply because of the basic conservatism and stability of utilities stocks.)

Probably sector funds are best left to

(1) very sophisticated investors, who believe that they can figure out in advance which industries will flourish for a while;

(2) investors who prefer owning stocks, not funds, but want more stability in their stock portfolios; and

(3) long-term investors who are of a mind that certain sectors will perform exceptionally well over the long run — health care, for example.

27

FIXED-INCOME FUNDS

In recent years, corporate bonds, municipal bonds, Ginnie Maes, U.S. Treasurys, and other fixed-income investments have become almost as volatile as stocks. Over the ten-year period from 1980 to 1991, for example, bonds appreciated as much as 31.09% in one year — and as little as 2.3% in another year.

Buying fixed-income investments, like corporate bonds, is not always a simple matter, either. The difference between what two different brokers may charge in commissions can be enormous. So can the "spread" — the difference between the "wholesale" price the brokerage firm pays for a bond and the "retail" price it charges you. You must also pay attention to "call" provisions (see below), credit ratings, and maturities.

You could, of course, just buy bonds of blue-chip companies, or high-rated municipals, or U.S. Treasurys — if you have $5000 or $10,000 — and hold on until the securities mature, hoping that inflation does not erode your principal. But you could make more money with a diversified portfolio that includes lower-rated bonds. And you'll be more insulated from fluctuating interest rates with a portfolio that includes bonds of different maturities. Finally, you can invest with only $500 or so. Hence, the case for using mutual funds.

In general, fixed-income investments are safer than investments in equities, or stocks. When you lend money by purchasing bonds or CDs, you're less likely to lose your principal, just as you're less likely to have your principal appreciate much before the loan comes due. (But in the world of investing, there are almost always exceptions. A low-rated bond may not be as safe as a blue-chip stock; long-term bonds — those that mature in ten years or more — may be more volatile than utilities or other conservative stocks.)

All loans are called "fixed-income" investments, though many yields are not really carved in stone. The interest rates on a money-market fund fluctuate from week to week; some notes have floating rates; even the yield on a unit investment trust (see below) can change as bonds are retired.

When you put money into mutual funds that invest primarily in bonds and other debt instruments, you always assume certain risks:

1. Rising interest rates — the longer a bond's maturity, the more the principal will erode if interest rates climb. A bond worth $1000 and paying 8% will be worth less on the market if interest rates rise to 9%. If interest rates remain high, the bond won't be worth the full $1000 until its maturity date.

2. Creditworthiness — the corporation may get into trouble (lawsuits, poor earnings, high debts), and its bonds may lose favor with investors, or even go into default.

3. Call provisions — if a bond can be called in at the end of ten years, and interest rates have declined, the issuer will pay off the bond holders (usually at a small premium) and leave them with the task of finding other bonds with high yields even though interest rates are low.

4. "Event" risk. A company may become the subject of a takeover bid or leveraged buyout involving additional debt, so that its existing bonds are downgraded.

The safest bond funds, obviously, are those that hold bonds with the shortest maturities, the highest ratings, and the strongest call protection. Most Treasurys cannot be called, and municipals rarely. Short-term bonds are generally considered those with maturities of less than three years; intermediate term, three to ten years; long-term, over ten years.

When you buy a standard open-end bond fund, you're sacrificing the assurance of getting your full principal back because the fund manager buys and sells bonds before maturity, perhaps even retreating entirely into cash, depending on where he or she thinks interest rates are going. But you gain the possibility of a higher yield and even capital gains. With an open-end bond fund, the minimum may be as low as $250, and you can sell at any time. Many funds have no sales charges. And any diversified basket of bonds can include some high-yield varieties, with the diversification protecting the fund in case of an occasional default.

You can buy funds based on their maturities or on the creditworthiness of their holdings. But you may have to phone a fund to learn the average maturity of its holdings or the grades of their securities — the name sometimes provides no clue, and the prospectus gives the fund lots of leeway. You can also invest in a flexible fund, where the manager can decide which maturities to emphasize.

Just don't make the horrendous mistake of buying a bond fund simply because of its higher yield, which can be a trap. Some funds with high yields have been losing principal. In one recent year, one bond fund had a yield of 14.5% and a total return of −6.4%, whereas another had a yield of 12.9% and a total return of 3%. You would have been 9.4 percentage points better off in the second, despite its lower yield. Before investing, examine a fund's track record.

By and large, you will be better off with a fund with a large asset base. It will have the clout to obtain the better securities, as well as the money to be widely diversified. Also pay attention to fund expenses. Because the yields from different bond funds aren't usually wide, funds that keep expenses low are likely to be among the leaders. Vanguard High Yield's expense ratio is usually around 0.4%, First Investors for Income, around 1.0%.

A *unit trust* will give you good diversification and the benefits of professionals picking the bonds to go into the trust. But there's little flexibility, since the trust holds the bonds until maturity, paying you interest over 1 to 30 years (depending on the trust) and then returning your principal. The minimum investment is usually $2500 to $5000. Stockbrokers charge a commission of 3–5%, but the management fee is minuscule because there is virtually no management. You cannot automatically reinvest distributions. You cannot switch in and out, as you can do with mutual funds. But you can sell your shares, for a profit or a loss, to the sponsor or to the trust.

Jane Bryant Quinn, the columnist, has shrewdly pointed out that no one really knows how well unit trusts have fared because no one has tracked them. And their performances may vary, depending on call provisions, whether bonds are sold to cover redemptions, whether any bonds default, and whether any bonds were purchased at a premium, in which case you get less than your investment at maturity.

28

MONEY MARKET FUNDS

Money-market mutual funds are like checking accounts — but, in most ways, much better.

Whatever money you put into such a fund, you will receive back. It's risk-free. (Well, almost risk-free — read on.) If you invest $1000, you will receive your $1000 back — tomorrow or 5 or 50 years down the road, at your choice. When professional investors talk of keeping some of their assets in "cash," they usually mean money-market funds.

Your $1000 has bought 1000 shares — the price of shares of almost all money market funds is almost always kept at $1. Meanwhile, your money earns interest — but the interest rate varies from week to week. These rates have almost always been higher than the rates you can receive from passbook savings accounts, NOW or super-NOW accounts, or money-market deposit accounts (what commercial banks and savings and loan associations call their own money-market funds). True, you may receive a higher interest rate if you invest in a six-month certificate of deposit, but you usually can't withdraw the money, without penalty, for six months.

Most money-market funds will provide you, free, with checks to use against your deposits. The minimum amount you can write may be $250 or $500. Most funds, again, don't set a limit on how many checks you can write, free of charge, within any time period. (Most money-market deposit accounts set a limit — like three checks a month.) There's also a minimum amount you need to set up a money-market fund: usually $250 to $500.

When you shop for a money-market fund, focus on the nterest rate — but also pay attention to the details about .heck-writing privileges and minimums. And keep in mind that, for absolute safety, a bank's money-market deposit account has an advantage: Government agencies insure the accounts at most banks and S&Ls for up to $100,000 each. A money-market mutual fund is usually not insured, though these funds invest in short-term U.S. government notes and bills; other very safe securities like $100,000-and-up ("jumbo") certificates of deposit offered by banks; and commercial paper — short-term obligations issued by corporations.

The first money-market fund — the Reserve Fund — was launched in 1972. Before then, only the rich could afford to invest huge amounts — $100,000 and more — in short-term debt instruments to capture high interest, while retaining their liquidity (ready access to their money) and safety of funds. Money-market funds have allowed ordinary investors to obtain high yields on their deposits, too, at the same time that their deposits remained accessible. Again, mutual funds have served as a means of democratizing the investment process.

These debt instruments don't extend more than an average of 90 days. Thus, the fund's principal is relatively stable: Normally you won't lose much if you had a 60-day note, interest rates rose, and you were forced to sell your note before 60 days had elapsed.

What money-market funds do to keep their principal absolutely unchanging is to vary the interest rate that shareholders receive. The rate changes from week to week, though usually these variations are tiny. Whereas your shares always should have a value of $1, your current yield may be 6.7% one week, 6.68% another week. And if interest rates start climbing, your yield will go up rather quickly, too.

Indeed, back in 1981, when inflation was raging, some funds were paying almost 18% a year. By the same token, when interest rates decline, money-market funds aren't especially desirable; at one point in the 1980s, money-market funds were paying the same rates you would get from a bank's passbook savings account.

Money-market funds can also invest in short-term tax-exempt securities issued by states, cities, and public authorities. Your interest will be less, but it will escape Federal taxation. If you invest in a fund that buys only the short-term securities issued in your home state, your interest may escape both Federal and state taxes. This is, of course, tempting for taxpayers who live in states with fairly high tax rates. Funds may also invest entirely in short-term Treasury securities, which are of course backed by the full faith and credit of the U.S. government, and which are also exempt from state taxes in most states.

Many investors mistakenly think that the yields on different money-market funds are so close that it isn't worth the bother of shopping around. While this may be true if you have only a few hundred dollars, it isn't true if you're handling sizable amounts of money for good periods of time. Year after year, certain money market funds pay higher rates than others. For example, if you invest $5000 in a fund yielding 5.25% a year, your investment would grow to $8423 over ten years. If the fund's yield was 6.25% a year, your $5000 would grow to $9296. The difference is $873, which would have gone a long way toward paying the taxes due on your fund's earnings. (See the box below.)

A fund can boost its yield by extending the maturity of the debt instruments in its portfolio or by buying Eurodollars, say, or low-grade commercial paper. Eurodollars are deposits in foreign branches of American banks. In an emergency — like a war — these deposits may be frozen. Commercial paper involves short-term loans to companies that need cash temporarily. Low-grade paper — issued by not-especially-prosperous companies — carries a small amount of risk.

If you're very worried about safety, stick with funds that

have net assets of $100 million or more; that buy debt with average maturities in line with those of other funds; and that do not buy Eurodollars or non-prime paper. Or just invest in money-market funds that buy government securities (Vanguard has one, and naturally it pays less).

But bear in mind that the last time any money-market mutual fund lost its investors any money was back in 1978. The manager of a tiny fund, First Multifund for Income, expected that interest rates would decline, so he extended his loans' average maturities to 650 days. Interest rates climbed. The fund's price per share fell below $1, to 93 cents. The fund liquidated, and its investors lost 7% of their principal. (Of course, for a time, the fund paid unusually high rates — because it had become, in effect, a short-term bond fund.)

THE DIFFERENCE THAT 1% MAKES

To figure out how much more you will earn on a money-market mutual fund that pays 1% or 2% more per year than another fund, check the table below. The table uses investments of $3000 and $5000 as examples. Thus, $3000 invested for 15 years at 5.25% will give you $6560. But $3000 invested at 6.25% will give you $7605 — a difference of $945.

Yield	Amount	1 Year	3 Years	5 Years	10 Years	15 Years
5.25%	$3,000	$3,161	$3,508	$3,894	$ 5,054	$ 6,560
	5,000	5,268	5,847	6,490	8,423	10,933
6.25%	3,000	3,192	3,613	4,091	5,578	7,605
	5,000	5,320	6,022	6,818	9,296	12,676
7.25%	3,000	3,223	3,722	4,297	6,154	8,814
	5,000	5,372	6,203	7,161	10,257	14,690

29

REAL ESTATE FUNDS

For profitability, real estate is a keen rival of a diversified basketful of common stocks. Well-chosen real estate — residential and commercial — has kept pace with the appreciation of stocks, and without their volatility. The drawback of most real-estate investments, of course, is their lack of liquidity. You can't quickly sell vacant land, a house, an industrial property, or a real-estate limited partnership — unless you're willing to lose a good deal of money.

Mutual funds may not be the best way to buy real estate, even though they do provide liquidity. Instead, you can buy real estate investment trusts — which are sold like stocks on exchanges. You will get a diversified selection of properties, mortgages, or both. The *Value Line Investment Survey,* which is available in large libraries, rates 13 REITs for safety and timeliness and also gives a periodic review of the industry. There are also many local, regional, and national limited partnerships that invest in real estate. REITs may be preferable, as a rule. They are much more liquid — you can sell a REIT just as you would sell a stock. And it's easier to choose a good REIT than a good limited partnership. Much more information is available about REITs.

A few mutual-fund companies have begun offering REITs

and limited partnerships. T. Rowe Price's limited partnerships and Vanguard's REIT are sold without the commissions normally charged.

A few mutual fund families have also recently begun offering funds that concentrate on real estate. Fidelity Real Estate and National Real Estate Stock invest in REITs as well as in stocks of companies directly or indirectly in real estate. Since they began a few years ago, these funds have not been paragons of performance. Perhaps they need more time to prove themselves. And the question has been raised about the wisdom of investing in a variety of real-estate ventures via mutual funds versus investing in the variety you can obtain from an individual REIT. T. Rowe Price and Vanguard, after all, are rather smart mutual-fund companies, yet they chose the REIT and limited-partnership routes, not a mutual fund.

A final possibility: asset-allocation funds that include real estate in their holdings. Among them are USAA Cornerstone (no-load; 800-531-8000 — in Texas, 512-498-8000; $1000 minimum); Permanent Portfolio (no-load; 800-531-5241; in Texas, 512-453-7558; $1000 minimum); and BB & K Diversa (no-load; 415-571-6002; $25,000 minimum).

30

PRECIOUS METALS FUNDS

"Become a bullionaire!" proclaims a circular being mailed around the country. And these days even many shrewd investment advisers urge that everyone have 5% to 15% of their portfolios in gold, or in precious metals in general.

But many other professional investors are dubious. Over the long run, gold has not fared very well. Lexington Goldfund's average annualized return over the past ten years has been a mere 1.95%. And that's one of the better precious-metals funds.

To invest in gold, you can buy the bullion itself; you can buy gold certificates from a dealer, stockbroker, or banker; you can buy coins; or you can buy the stocks of gold-mining companies. Generally, these stocks climb faster when gold is in demand—and sink faster when demand falters. South African mining companies pay higher dividends than domestic or other foreign companies, but in the long run their stocks are risky because of the country's racial troubles.

Finally, you can buy gold through mutual funds. Some invest exclusively in gold-mining companies; others invest in gold bullion as well, which may give a portfolio more stability; still others invest in silver and platinum, thus providing more diversity.

Investors interested in owning gold might be best advised to look for a fund with a good record, a fund that can invest in bullion, silver, and platinum, and that invests in both South Africa and in other countries. Four such funds are listed below.

Fund	Return*	800 Number
Bull & Bear Gold	7.18%	847-4200
Fidelity Precious Metals (3% Load)	7.75%	544-6666
Lexington Goldfund	10.10%	526-0057
Vanguard Gold	13.27%	362-0530

*Annual Return, 1985–1990

Probably an even better way to invest in gold is via an asset-allocation fund, such as Blanchard Strategic Growth, Permanent Portfolio, or USAA Cornerstone.

31

FAMILIES OF FUNDS

There's no official definition of *family* as the word is applied to mutual funds, though it obviously means a large number of funds under one umbrella. An attempt at a strict definition: a group of funds that includes one stock fund, one bond fund, and one money-market fund. The largest family is Fidelity Investments, which has over 100 different funds.

A family provides benefits. You can switch from one fund to another with a minimum of red tape. Your records will be simpler. If you want to flee from stocks to cash, all you need do is have your shares transferred to a sister money-market fund. Still, there's no reason to buy shares of a mediocre member of a distinguished family.

Occasionally someone rates the various families. Here are the no-load or low-load funds top-ranked (as of 1991) by Kanon Bloch Carré in Boston, a brokerage firm that trades exclusively in mutual funds:

1. Fidelity Investments; 2. Vanguard Group; 3. Phoenix Group; 4. American Funds; 5. Federated Management; 6. Scudder Funds; 7. Merrill Lynch; 8. Investment Advisers; 9. Columbia Funds; and 10. Smith Barney Advisers.

32

NONDIVERSIFIED FUNDS

It will surprise even serious students of mutual funds that some of them are nondiversified. As defined by the Securities and Exchange Commission, to be classified as "diversified" a fund must keep 75% of its assets diversified, so that no more than 5% of its assets are in the securities of one company.

But funds can obtain permission to be labeled "nondiversified," in which case only 50% of their assets need be diversified, and up to 25% of their net assets can be in a single company. (Many new funds begin as nondiversified, just to obtain time to build up their holdings.)

Running a nondiversified fund, portfolio managers need not spread themselves too thin. Some nondiversified funds have as few as eight or ten stocks. The manager can concentrate his or her attention on a limited basketful of securities. But if the portfolio manager makes a few mistakes, shareholders may suffer mightily.

As you would have guessed, nondiversified funds include a few of the very best performers, a few average performers, and a disproportionate share of the real stinkers. Their betas, naturally, tend to be high.

Some funds, by the way, are officially "nondiversified" but nonetheless hold a wide selection of securities. Hartwell Emerging Growth, for example, recently held 28 stocks in a variety of industries. Contrast that with Sherman Dean, which held 13.

You can usually tell how well diversified a fund is by checking its R squared, a measure of a fund's diversification. R squared (coefficient of determination) is the percentage of a fund's ups-and-downs that can be attributed to the movement of the stock market itself. A fund with an R squared of 100 is as diversified as the Standard & Poor's 500. (Not surprisingly, Vanguard Index-500 has an R squared of 100.) A well-diversified fund like Fidelity Magellan has an R squared of 94; a nondiversified fund like Sherman Dean, 45; an extremely nondiversified fund like Fidelity Select-Energy, 16.

Of course, the R squared is not an infallible measure of a fund's stability. Valley Forge is one of the most conservative of all funds. It's really a money-market fund masquerading as a stock fund. Once in a while, it launches a foray into an underpriced blue-chip stock, makes a killing, and quickly retreats. It has an R squared of 53.

Should you ever consider a nondiversified fund? Certainly if it's a fund with Sequoia's or Constellation's glittering record, or if it's as conservatively managed as Valley Forge.

33

INDEX FUNDS

Indexes are replicas of the stock market, or of any other market, as a whole. The most famous index, the Dow Jones Industrial Average, contains 30 blue-chip stocks. As an index, it's crude but useful. It doesn't reflect what is happening among small-company stocks. And it exaggerates the market's movements. The Standard & Poor's 500 Stock Index is preferred by professional investors, but it, too, is skewed toward big-company stocks. Other indexes — the Wilshire 5000, the Value Line Composite — are less well-known, but they give a more comprehensive picture of what the market as a whole has been doing.

Index funds are modeled on a market index, typically the S&P 500. Generally, they perform a little worse than the index, because they have more expenses (it costs money to buy and sell stocks according to their representation in the S&P 500).

Here's a sobering fact: Stock index funds tend to do better than 75% of all mutual funds. Bond index funds tend to do better than 80% of all mutual funds. Why invest in anything but an index fund, then? An index fund like Vanguard's 500 is no-load; it has a zero management fee; its expense ratio is a tiny 0.22%; its turnover is low. And its ten-year average annualized return has been 13.47%; its five-year return, 12.78%; its three-year return, 13.86%. Its beta, of course, is 1. And you get extraordinary diversification.

Despite these advantages, most investors are reluctant to invest in an index fund. Perhaps because it's hard to accept doing only average. Or because owning an index fund is dull. Watching your fund compete against the averages is much more fun. Finally, for a sophisticated investor, it's easy to resist buying shares of an index fund when there are other funds, like Fidelity Magellan and the 20th Century Growth Fund that over time beat the S&P 500 by a good margin.

Still, older investors, conservative investors, might think about an index fund. Kevin Johnson, Vanguard 500's former portfolio manager, suggested putting 70% of your stock portfolio into his fund and 30% into more aggressive funds.

While Vanguard's was the first index fund open to the public, such funds have begun to proliferate. A replica of Vanguard's index is the Colonial U.S. Equity Index Trust; why anyone would buy it over Vanguard's is a mystery, because it has a 5.75% sales charge. There's also a fund that invests in the 10% of New York Stock Exchange issues with the lowest market capitalizations. And even Vanguard has come out with a new index fund, the Extended Market Portfolio. It tries to duplicate the investment results of small-company stocks (those not included in the S&P 500), using the Wilshire 4500 index as a model, but with fewer stocks. (The Wilshire 4500 is the Wilshire 5000 without the S&P 500.)

34

ETHICAL FUNDS

Sometimes mutual funds seem to give investors *too* many choices, and that seems to be the case with "ethical" or "socially responsible" funds.

Such funds may avoid investing in tobacco and liquor companies, in companies with nuclear-power plants, in companies with strained labor relations, in companies that deal with South Africa, in companies that make weapons, or in companies that pollute the environment.

No two ethical funds seem to have the same "screens." And not much love is lost among the different funds.

The intriguing question about such funds is whether they perform any better, or worse, than other funds.

As of this writing, many of the ethical funds are doing very well. Probably the main reason is that small-company stocks are thriving, and this is where the smaller ethical funds generally invest. But advocates of the funds claim that they will always do especially well. After all, they avoid troubled companies — like those with nuclear power, those that grow tobacco, those with strained labor-management relations and that are therefore more susceptible to strikes.

The opposing arguments: Success in the market is usually the result of buying stocks low — whatever the companies behind the stocks; focusing on ethical investments narrows your investment universe; it also serves as a distraction.

A simple way to resolve the argument is to examine the long-term record of two of the oldest ethical funds: Dreyfus Third Century (1972) and Pioneer (1928), which doesn't trumpet itself as an ethical fund.

Since they began, both funds have been strikingly average performers.

The message seems to be that ethical funds are for ethical people — not necessarily for investors seeking the highest possible returns. Sheldon Jacobs, editor of *The Handbook for No-Load Fund Investors,* dismisses ethical funds this way: "Given their relative unattractiveness, investors might consider putting their money into better-performing funds and giving the additional profits to their favorite charity."

Ethical funds include Calvert Social Investment in Washington, D.C.; Dreyfus Third Century, in New York City; New Alternatives in Great Neck, N.Y.; Pax World, in Portsmouth, N.H.; Pioneer, Pioneer II, and Pioneer III of Boston; and the Parnassus Fund of San Francisco.

35

NEW FUNDS

Throughout the land, very intelligent and imaginative people are thinking up ideas for new mutual funds. Like a new invention, or a new type of business, a new and truly needed fund can be an avenue to money and fame.

The question is whether an investor should ever put money into a new fund. There is, after all, a powerful argument against it: The new fund has no track record. Yet there are fine funds that have been around for 3, 5, 10, 20, and 30 years.

Certainly you should not buy new closed-end stock funds — their prices almost invariably plummet. You also should be skeptical of new open-end funds, and probably never put any significant amounts of money into them, but you might want to consider such funds under certain circumstances.

1. A successful fund has been closed to new investors but its managers have opened a "clone" fund.

These clone funds tend to do almost as well, or as well, as their older, bigger models. The new portfolio managers probably have learned at the feet of the masters, and while the two may not buy identical securities, they probably buy clone securities.

Nicholas Limited Edition (net assets: $70.9 million) has

actually fared far better than its older sibling (net assets: $1.3 billion) since it began, although both are managed by Albert Nicholas. (Nicholas has never closed its doors, by the way.) The three-year annualized return of Limited is 13.65%, as against Nicholas's 11.84%. That is an argument in favor of switching out of an older, gargantuan fund when it launches a similar new fund.

2. The investment company launching the fund has a fine record.

Many rookie funds that do splendidly during their first years are the offspring of famous families. The companies behind them were probably blessed not just with talent and experience, but a knowledge of what kind of new fund might sparkle.

3. The manager of the new fund has a fine record managing money.

It would surely be tempting to buy shares of a fund managed by such financial wizards as J.P. Morgan or Bernard Baruch. There are many contemporary money managers of great skill. Who could doubt, for instance, that Mario Gabelli would make a success of Gabelli Asset, considering that he has been No. 1 year after year in managing money for private accounts?

Still, one must remember horrifying exceptions: A noted investment adviser, Gerald Tsai, lost a lot of his shareholders' money after launching his first mutual fund in the 1960s.

4. The new fund has a shrewd new approach that fits in with some of your own thinking.

Take the new asset-allocation funds. USAA Cornerstone, for example, shifts its investments among U.S. stocks, foreign securities, precious metals securities, and fixed-income securities—a system many people have come to like. For safety, there are minimum and maximum levels within each sector—so the fund will never be, say, 100% into precious metals. USAA Cornerstone ended the difficult year of 1987 with a total return of 9%.

36

SIZE AND PERFORMANCE

A fund's assets — money under management — minus its current debts (taxes and other operating expenses) make up its net assets.

The net assets of a fund that has been flourishing will usually grow, simply because more and more investors will move into that fund.

At the end of 1986, the net assets of the Mathers Fund were $134.8 million. During 1987, the fund's total return was a delightful 27% — the fund had retreated into cash before the crash. By the middle of 1988, the fund's assets had grown to $190.6 million. Another growth fund, Seligman Capital, went the other way, from $186.7 to $140.5 million, when its total return plunged by 29% during the same period.

Naturally, the best-performing funds tend to be large. (These days, $250 million is considered medium-sized for an aggressive-growth fund, $500 million for a growth fund.) Investors flock to them. But that leads to the intriguing question: Once a fund gets to be large, does its performance suffer?

Generally, the answer of the experts is Yes. Muscle-bound funds cannot buy small issues and make enormous profits — because they would move the price of such stocks too far up. And the large funds are leery of buying into small-capitalization stocks anyway, because if they decided to sell, they would drive the prices down.

Also, a large fund cannot quickly shift its holdings to take advantage of changes. When Fidelity Equity Income (net assets: $4 billion) wants to buy $75 million worth of a stock (a typical holding for a fund of its size), it usually can purchase $1 million a day without unduly driving up the price. So the fund needs 75 days to move into a stock — and 75 business days to move out. On the other hand, a small fund can buy small-company stocks as well as large ones — and turn on a dime.

Should you, then, stick with stock funds that have less than $250 million in assets? The answer is No.

If you had followed that strategy in recent years, you would have been very sorry. From 1983 until the beginning of 1991, blue-chip stocks were on a tear — while small-company stocks languished. Blue chips did well because foreigners were more interested in them, and because of the proliferation of index funds, which typically buy the blue-chip stocks that make up the leading indexes.

Besides, the best portfolio managers and analysts tend to wind up at the gigantic funds. These funds become gigantic because of their expertise; and because their employers have huge assets, they are better paid — and they get more acclaim from the public and from their peers.

A giant fund will also have the clout to buy shares of an attractive new issue. New England Growth (assets: $614 million) was able to buy shares of a high-flier like Home Shopping Network; a smaller fund, Hartwell Emerging Growth (assets: $25 million), was not.

The best reason to consider giant funds, though, is given by Michael Price of Mutual Shares. The more assets you have, the more you can afford to hire new analysts in new areas—and the more undervalued stocks you can find. This helps balance things out.

Certainly, despite its elephantine clumsiness, Fidelity Equity Income—along with Magellan and Puritan—continues to do well. So do Vanguard Windsor and Windsor II, Wellington, and Mutual Shares. One reason is that they can afford a flock of top-flight analysts, and therefore have access to the most timely, reliable information.

With fixed-income funds and money-market funds, you're probably best advised to favor those with the greatest assets. Such funds have more clout and can buy the most attractive new issues. They can also diversify more. On the other hand, if you have a choice between two growth funds with similar records, you should probably tilt toward the one with lower net assets.

37

NET ASSET VALUES

The net asset value, or NAV, of a mutual fund is the fund's price per share. For most money-market funds, for example, the NAV is kept at $1, and $1000 will buy you 1000 shares.

With *no-load funds,* you pay the NAV when you buy shares. If you invest $1000 in a typical no-load stock fund with an NAV of $15, you will own 66.67 shares ($1000 divided by $15).

With *load funds,* the sales commission determines how many shares you will wind up with for, say, $1000. If the load is 8.5%, $85 of your $1000 goes for sales commissions; if the NAV is $15, the "offering price" would be 16.393 ($15 divided by 91.5%). You would wind up with 61 shares ($1000 divided by 16.393). Or divide $915 by $15 to get 61 shares.

You calculate the asset value by taking the value of the securities that a fund is managing and dividing that figure by the number of shares outstanding. If a fund's net assets are $10 million, and there are 500,000 shares held by investors, the NAV is $20.

The NAV fluctuates from day to day, mainly depending on how the securities the fund owns have performed the previous day. It also fluctuates because of withdrawals to pay fund expenses, and occasionally because of distributions—

when the fund passes along capital gains, dividends, and interest to its shareholders.

The actual NAV has little significance to the average investor, though it can be suggestive.

When a fund is first made available to investors, its managers decide on an offering price per share. The number is arbitrary, but usually it's $10.

But when one gold fund was first offered, its price was set at $1—to suggest that the fund was speculative.

A high net asset value, on the other hand, may indicate conservatism. Recently the NAV of Endowments, Inc., a growth-and-income fund for tax-exempt institutions, was around $1676, just before a 100-to-1 split. When the fund was launched in 1970, the NAV was set at $1000 per share—so that "investors would not think that this was play money," a spokesperson explains.

Beyond that, a fund with a very low NAV may not have performed well—and a fund with a high NAV may have been outstanding. Steadman Associated's NAV was recently $0.61; Fidelity Magellan's, $65.

But this is not an infallible guide. The number depends not only on the fund's performance but also on how long the fund has been in existence, whether the original NAV was $10, and whether or not the fund has ever split its shares (giving investors two shares for the price of one, say, and cutting the net asset value in half).

38

DISTRIBUTIONS

Any money that a mutual fund directs your way is a "distribution," including:

• dividends from common and preferred stocks.

• interest from bonds and Treasury obligations — which, confusingly, are classified as "dividends."

• net realized capital gains — profits from assets that went up in value before being sold, minus losses from assets that declined in value before being sold (*realized* means that the securities were sold; you don't owe capital gains taxes on securities you haven't sold, even if their value has grown).

• tax-exempt interest dividends — you now report them on Form 1040, though they are usually still not taxed.

• return of capital — nontaxable disbursements, because you're getting back your principal. (Sometimes these distributions are called "tax-free dividends.")

• undistributed capital gains — in rare instances, a fund pays taxes on its gains even before selling the securities. You must pay taxes on the gains the fund allocated to you, even though you didn't receive them.

What sort of distributions you will receive from a fund depends on the fund. Aggressive-growth and growth stock funds will bless you, if you're lucky, with mostly capital gains; stock income and fixed-income funds will give you dividends, interest, or both.

Mutual funds themselves do not pay taxes on any capital gains, interest, or dividends they receive from their holdings because they disburse almost all of these gains to their shareholders. They are merely a conduit. But to continue to qualify as a nontaxable conduit, during a calendar year they must distribute most of their net realized gains and income dividends.

When you buy shares of a mutual fund, you are asked to make a choice: Do you want your distributions reinvested in more shares; or do you want them mailed to you? Do you want capital gains mailed to you, and dividends reinvested— or vice versa?

Most shareholders—around 80%—reinvest all their distributions. It's a good way to obtain more shares automatically, as well as to practice a rough version of dollar-cost averaging.

In general, it's not a good idea to buy shares of a fund just before a distribution. You will receive part of your investment back—and it will now be taxable. Even if you directed that your distributions be reinvested, you will owe a tax. (But by paying taxes on these distributions, the "basis"—cost for tax purposes—of your new shares will be different.)

Most funds make distributions in December, and some also make them in July. Phone a fund to make sure you aren't investing just before a distribution. If you're investing only a small amount of money, though, and you're eager to own shares, you might plunge ahead. The tax liability will usually be small.

39

EX-DIVIDEND DATES

The term "ex-dividend" comes from the stock market. When a stock issues its dividend, its price generally goes down, to reflect the disbursement. Buyers of *new* shares on or after that day aren't entitled to that dividend.

The term has been carried over to mutual funds, but here the term "ex-distribution" would be more suitable. After all, a fund supposedly can go "ex-dividend" when it distributes capital gains as well as dividends.

Some newspaper listings do distinguish between "ex-dividend" ("x") and "ex-distribution" ("d"). In this case, "ex-distribution" means capital gains, or capital gains as well as dividends.

On a fine spring day recently, many newspapers published the following in their mutual-fund listings:

	NAV	Offer Price	NAV Chg.
Nicholas	xd 31.72	N.L.	− .38

On that day, about 300 alert shareholders phoned the Nicholas Fund to ask either, Why had the fund lost so much money? or, What was the distribution?

Novices asked the first question, veterans asked the second.

The fund, of course, had gone ex-dividend or ex-distribution. It had parceled out most of its net profits from securities it had sold earlier in the year, along with accumulated dividends and interest. Shareholders who wanted those distributions reinvested now owned more shares, at a price of $31.72 apiece. Those who wanted the distributions mailed to them received a check.

But unless they telephoned the fund, shareholders didn't know what their holdings were worth now or how much money they would receive. They would not know until the following week, when they received a mailing from the fund.

The reason is that the "−.38" was a combination of two numbers. One was for the money set aside for the distribution, representing (as it happened) −.57 of the fund's net asset value per share. The other number was +.19, the amount that the fund's NAV had risen the previous day. Together, they added up to the −.38 change listed in the newspaper.

To learn what their holdings were worth now, shareowners could

• multiply the number of shares they owned before the distribution by 32.29 (31.72 + .57); or

• multiply the new number of shares they now owned by 31.72. The new number is the old number they owned, plus (the older number times .57 divided by 31.72).

Of course, as long as they were phoning Nicholas to learn what the distribution was, they could also ask what their current holdings were worth.

Newspapers get their data from the wire services — Associated Press or United Press — which, in turn, get them from Nasdaq, the National Associated Securities Dealers Automated Quotation system. Nasdaq does provide a breakdown of the change in the net asset value, but newspapers don't use it, claiming that they lack the space. But they could easily print the distributions at the bottom of the listings.

40

MONITORING
PERFORMANCE

You can check how your funds are performing from day to day by looking at the Mutual Funds listings in any large newspaper.

But to check how your funds are faring compared with other funds, or how they have performed over a month, three months, or longer, you should subscribe to a mutual-funds newsletter or a financial magazine.

Below is what you are likely to see in a newspaper:

Mutual Funds			
	NAV	*Buy*	*Chg.*
AcornF	39.10	NL	+.16
AlgerG t	10.13	10.13	−.01
American Cap:			
Cmstk	...	...	...
Dreyfus Grp:			
CapV p	24.30	25.45	+.14
Fidelity Invest:			
CapAp r	13.53	13.81	+.05
Nicholas Group:			
NchInc x	3.74	NL	−.09

NAV means "net asset value"—the price per share of a fund. A share of Acorn was worth $39.10 on that day.

Buy or *Offer Price* is the amount you pay per share of a fund. For a share of Acorn, you would pay $39.10, the NAV, because it's a no-load (NL) fund—there is no sales charge.

Chg means "change"—the difference between NAV at the end of the previous day and the day before. Acorn, a fund that owns many small-company stocks, gained about 0.41% (0.16 divided by [$39.10 minus 0.16, or $38.94, the NAV two days before]). The Dow Jones Industrial Average had gained 0.75%; the Nasdaq index of mostly small-company stocks had fallen 0.02%, while American Stock Exchange issues had inched up 0.38%. So Acorn did a little better than the Amex.

Alger Growth has a deferred sales charge—a back-end load. (It's 5% the first year and vanishes after six years.) That's why its NAV is identical with its *Buy* price, yet it's not listed as a no-load. The *t* means that the fund has both a 12b-1 distribution fee and either a redemption fee or deferred sales charge.

American Capital is a family of funds, including American Capital Comstock. None of the numbers for yesterday's session were available.

Dreyfus Capital Value has a 12b-1 or distribution plan—hence the *p*. The fund has a 4.5% sales charge, or load ($25.45 minus $24.30 is $1.15, divided by $25.45 is 4.5%).

Fidelity Capital Appreciation has a 2% sales charge along with a redemption fee (*r*) of 1%, so that the sales charge is, in effect, 3%. (Recently it dropped the redemption fee and raised the sales charge to 3%.)

The Nicholas Income Fund went ex-dividend on the previous day (*x*). A portion of the fund's recent dividend and interest income was set aside, either to be paid to shareholders or to be reinvested for them. To find out what the dividend amounted to, you would have to phone the fund: The "−.09" subtracted from the NAV also included any gain or loss in the NAV during the previous day.

If a fund had distributed capital gains and not dividends or interest, it might have had a *d* after its name, for "distribution," or an *e* for "ex-capital gains distribution."

The symbol *f* (not shown above) means that the figures are for the day before. (Funds that invest in other funds, for example, are always a day late in reporting their figures.) And *s* means that the shares have split — if you had owned 20 shares, you now might have 30 or 40.

Some newspapers use different symbols. And some just list the new NAV — you need the listings from the previous day to see how your fund has fared.

To be listed by the National Association of Securities Dealers, a fund must have 1,000 shareholders or $25 million in net assets. That's why you may not find a new fund listed, even though it may have a superlative performance record.

41

FIGURING OUT
THE YIELD

Your yield usually means the income you can pretty much count on receiving from an investment.

With mutual funds, though, the meaning of the word is a little slippery — and it can be very misleading.

If you invest in a certificate of deposit, you usually get an **un**varying yield — say, 7% for a one-year CD. But the yield from a mutual fund of different stocks, bonds, or both will vary continuously, as the individual stocks and bonds go up or down in price.

Here's how the 12-month yield is calculated:

Add all income distributions — dividends, interest, or both, but not capital gains — for the preceding 12 months. Then divide by the current net asset value (minus capital gains distributions). Capital gains or losses aren't part of the yield — they aren't regular or predictable. But they do constitute part of the total return — your yield *plus* gains or losses on your principal.

Before the Securities and Exchange Commission cracked down, some funds were advertising weekly or monthly yields, and some were including capital gains as well as irregular and unpredictable option income. Now advertised yields must be uniform.

111

Funds with the highest yields tend to hold bonds, high-dividend stocks, or both.

Buying a fund simply because of its high yield can be a terrible mistake. Recall the story about the man who was on vacation, driving across the country. He turned to his wife next to him and joyfully told her, "I'm lost, but — I'm making great time!" With a high-yielding fund, you can be making great time, heading directly for the poorhouse.

When you invest, you don't just want sizable regular distributions; you also want your original investment to retain its value, or even appreciate, and certainly not sink.

A stock's yield depends on both its price and its regular dividend. If a stock's price is $25 a share, and its regular dividend is 50 cents per share a quarter, your yield is 8%. (The dividend is $2 a year; divide $2 by $25.) But if the company's profits begin vanishing, investors will sell the stock. Its price might drop to $20 a share. That means that its yield grows to 10%. This isn't cause for rejoicing: The value of your shares has dropped 20%. And there's a danger that the company, pressed for cash, will cut its dividend. The same is true of the bonds issued by a company in trouble — their prices may sink, and their yields climb.

In short, a big yield can be a sign of big trouble.

The same is true of a mutual fund with a high yield. Its stocks or bonds may be on the fringes of financial stability. A bond fund may own low-rated, "junk" bonds; a stock fund may own issues with a high yield only because their prices are in the basement. Yet a high yield isn't always cause for alarm. A stock or bond fund may have so many different risky securities that some of the overall risk is diversified away.

To determine whether a fund's high yield means that it carries high risk, check its total return, too. The total return takes into consideration what is happening to your principal.

In a money-market fund, a high yield may mean that a fund is efficient; or it may mean that the fund owns short-term instruments with unusually long maturities — and if interest rates suddenly rise, that fund may be in for a long spell of below-average yields.

42

DECIPHERING
THE PROSPECTUS

A mutual fund cannot sell you shares unless it sends you a prospectus. (And if you become a shareholder, it must also send you updated prospectuses.) If you just send in a check asking to buy shares, the fund may invest the money on the day it comes in, sending you a prospectus and an application form when it mails back a confirmation of your investment. (But at least one fund, Lindner, will mail back your check if you haven't submitted an application form.)

The cover of the prospectus usually tells you a fund's investment objective (high income, capital gains, etc.); sales or redemption charges; minimums for first and repeat investments; retirement plans available; address and phone number.

Inside the prospectus is a table of all fees, charges, and operating expenses. The Securities and Exchange Commission now requires funds to show how much these fees and charges cost an investor if he or she redeems the shares at the end of one year, three years, five years, and ten years—assuming a first investment of $1000 and a 5% growth rate (rather low). Usually you'll also find financial statements—income and capital charges per share, expenses, net realized and unrealized gains or losses, distributions, and so forth.

The Investment Company Institute suggests that, in reading a prospectus, you concentrate on

• Date of issuance. Make sure you have the most recent edition (prospectuses must be updated every 16 months).

• Minimum investment

• Objective

• Record of performance

• Degree of risk

• Special features—like check-writing, telephone exchange, automatic investing.

• Fees

Also pay particular attention to the section in the prospectus describing how to redeem your shares. Remember how much you can withdraw by letter without a signature guarantee.

If you request it, you can also receive a Statement of Additional Information, which elaborates on the prospectus itself.

The prospectus is a formidably boring piece of literature. And it doesn't tell you what you probably are burning to know: how this fund has fared over the years in comparison with similar funds. You can get that information by reading a newsletter or a financial magazine.

In fact, if reading the entire prospectus is just too painful for you, you can make do with a description of the fund in updated books like the *Mutual Fund Sourcebook* and *The Handbook for No-Load Fund Investors*. (See the Introduction.) Such books will also give you important information missing in most prospectuses, such as who the fund's portfolio manager is and how volatile the fund has been.

43

INVESTMENT MINIMUMS

While a few funds have no minimum initial investment at all—you can even send in a dollar or two—most set a minimum, typically of $1000 or $2500. The minimum needed for subsequent investments is usually smaller—$50, $100, $250.

For novice investors and for the less well-to-do, a low minimum is a help. It's difficult to practice dollar-cost-averaging if you must begin investing in, say, Mutual Shares with $5000. A low minimum is especially suitable for children, to get them into the habit of investing in mutual funds with small amounts.

The minimum for an Individual Retirement Account is usually less than the minimum for an ordinary investment—$250 may be typical. Funds think that IRA money will remain in the fund for a long time, so they encourage contributions. But many funds charge a little extra—$5 or $10 a year—to handle an IRA.

Most funds prefer high minimums, simply because there's less paperwork—fewer mailings, fewer calculations—if the fund deals with fewer shareholders, who own relatively large numbers of shares. Perhaps funds also think that small investors are more likely to sell their shares in a general market decline, thus forcing a fund to sell its holdings at low prices. Michael Price of Mutual Shares, for example, suspects that shareholders in one of his funds, Beacon, are shrewder and less likely to panic and sell in a market downturn: Beacon's minimum is $50,000.

Among the funds with the lowest minimums is 20th Century Investors. Says its president, James Stowers, "We want to give everyone a chance." At the opposite pole, 20 money-market funds run by Keystone Custodian require initial minimum investments of $75 million. These funds are for institutional investors, such as pension plans, but if you yourself sent in $75 million, they might deign to accept it.

Fund families tend to have similar minimums and followups. Older funds also tend to have lower minimums.

Here are some of the better-performing funds, their minimums, and their minimums for reinvestments:

Fund	Initial Minimum	Followups
Dreyfus Capital Value	$2,500	$100
Fidelity Magellan	2,500	250
Manhattan	1,000	100
Nicholas	500	100
Price International	2,500	100
20th Century Select	None	None
Wellesley Income	3,000	100

44

BUY AND HOLD STRATEGIES

The most popular strategy for investing in stock and bond funds is to buy those with superior track records (and continuity of good management) and hold on. This tack is opposed to the market-timing approach and to momentum-following.

Market-timers scoff at buy-and-holders. "I invest on the assumption that the following year will be the worst that the stock market has seen for 20 years — and on the assumption that it will be my last year in the market," says market-timer Paul A. Merriman, an investment adviser in Seattle. "So, if the market gives signals of a major decline, it's too risky to remain invested." Merriman got out of the market in 1987, before the crash.

A momentum-follower, Burton Berry, a newsletter publisher in San Francisco, is contemptuous of buy-and-holding: "It's completely out of date. The market is so dynamic and volatile that buy-and-holders will someday wake up and find that their funds are dogs. Their head-in-the-sand belief that long-term records are reliable guides to the future is incredible."

But, as is true throughout the world of mutual funds, the term "buy and hold" is so broad that it can be misleading.

Many buy-and-holders aren't strict buy-and-holders. They would not dream of buying a fund like 44 Wall Street on the strength of a recent fine record, and holding their shares while the fund went into a seemingly permanent tailspin. Most buy-and-holders don't hold on forever.

When do these flexible buy-and-holders sell? When an aggressive-growth fund has underperformed similar funds for one or two years. When a growth or growth-and-income fund has lagged similar funds for two to three years.

Very likely, flexible buy-and-holders also engage in a bit of market-timing. Perhaps they buy funds whose managers tilt toward market-timing—the Rightime funds, Mathers. Perhaps they dollar-cost-average, which is a milk-and-water version of market-timing. Perhaps they follow the formula approach, keeping a certain percentage of their overall portfolio in stocks—raising it when their holdings (and the market) are down, pruning back when their holdings (and the market) are up. Or they may just lighten up a bit when they think the market is high, load up a bit when they think the market is low.

45

DOLLAR-COST AVERAGING

"Dollar-cost averaging" means diversifying the prices at which you buy an investment over a period of time—so you wind up paying average or below-average prices. You try to "average" the "dollar-cost" of your securities.

Mutual funds can help you diversify your overall portfolio and your subportfolios. But it's up to you to diversify the prices you pay for any investments.

If you invest a large sum all at once, you may pay too high a price—and wait a very long time before your original investment begins appreciating. If you had bought Fidelity Magellan on January 1, 1987, by the end of the year you would have been ahead by 0.96%. If you had bought all your shares in early October, by the end of the year you would have sustained a loss of almost 25%.

Many amateur investors buy shares in a mutual fund; they watch in dismay as the net asset value (NAV) slowly sinks; then, when the price finally climbs up to their original purchase price, they sell, breathing a sigh of relief.

Logically, you would think that if you staggered your investments, you would wind up with an average price. The truth is more pleasant. By staggering your investments, you wind up with a below-average price. The reason is that if you invest a fixed sum at regular intervals, when the fund price is low, you will be able to buy more shares.

Let's say that a fund is selling at a net asset value of $15. In

119

three months, the price sinks to $10. Three months later, it climbs to $25. Three months after that, it drops to $20. Add up the prices ($70) and divide by four: The average share price is $17.50.

Suppose that during this same period you buy $2000 worth of shares every three months—133.34 shares at $15, 200 at $10, 80 at $25, and 100 at $20. Divide the number of shares you have bought (513.34) into $8000. Your average purchase price is $15.58—less than the average price of $17.50.

Of course, while dollar-cost averaging can prevent disaster, it can also reduce your winnings. If the shares' price had gone up for the entire year, you would be cursing the notion of dollar-cost averaging. But if the price had sunk, at least your average price for those shares would have been lower than it could have been.

While dollar-cost averaging can be suitable for other types of investments besides mutual funds, it works best for securities that are volatile, but tend to wind up higher over the course of time—like stocks. If you happen to stagger your investments into a mutual fund that keeps going down, you will wind up with smaller losses than otherwise—but losses nonetheless. Dollar-cost averaging is no substitute for choosing a good mutual fund to begin with.

46

FORMULA INVESTING

An alternative to dollar-cost averaging is formula investing. It's another way of trying to ensure that you buy low and sell high.

Let's say that you have decided to apportion your overall portfolio into 50% stock mutual funds, 35% fixed-income securities, and 15% cash equivalents. Then the stock market soars, and your stock funds now constitute 70% of your overall portfolio. So you sell a portion of your stock funds and apportion the profit among your other portfolios, bringing them back up to par. You are probably better off selling the funds in which you have the least confidence. (You could sell the funds that have made you the most money, but that might not be wise. After all, if the portfolio manager has done well, why not stick with a winner?)

But suppose that your stock funds have declined, and now constitute only 25% of your overall portfolio. Now you sell a portion of your fixed-income securities, and dip into your cash, to bring everything back to 50-35-10 again.

This 25%-up, 20%-down formula is flexible; you could use larger or smaller percentages. But don't use the same percentages — 25% and 25%, for example. If the value of your stock funds falls 25%, you're now dealing with a smaller figure, and you would need an increase greater than 25% to bring the stock funds back up to 50% of your portfolio. (100 plus 25% is 125; 100 minus 25% is 75; 75 plus 25% is only 93.75.) So make your downside percentage smaller than your upside percentage. It might be 5% up, 4% down.

Another way to accomplish this task is not to realign your portfolio only in response to set percentages like 25% gains and 20% declines in your stock holdings. Instead, every three to six months, say, you bring your percentages back into line. If your stock funds are 55% of your overall portfolio after three months, you cut back, for example. If they constitute 47%, you buy more shares. Thus, even when the market is relatively quiet, you will be keeping your portfolio up to date at regular intervals.

Reminder: Don't start a formula plan from scratch. Ease into stock funds gradually — either by dollar-cost averaging or by waiting for a period of stabilization after a major market decline.

47

MARKET-TIMING

One of the fiercest controversies swirling around mutual-fund investing is whether or not market-timing works. As is often the case with controversies, both sides make good points, and the truth is probably subtle and shaded.

Market-timing means lightening up on certain investments when you think they are about to decline, or have just begun to decline, and loading up on certain investments when you think they are about to go up, or have just begun their ascent. A market-timer in blue-chip stocks, ideally, would have invested in August of 1982 and sold out in August of 1987.

Predictably, there is a continuum of market-timers. Over on one side are investors whose idea of market-timing is to have a mere 10% or 20% of their stock-market investments in cash if they're worried, as opposed to their usual strategy of being fully invested or having only 5% in cash. On the opposing side are the aggressive market-timers, who are 100% in cash when they think that stocks are in, or are entering, a bear market.

Making everything more confusing are the indirect market-timers. When they see relatively few undervalued securities, they stop buying and build up their cash reserves. They claim they aren't market-timers, but they sure quack like them.

Most of the best-performing funds over the years have not been market-timers. Why? One possible answer is that, by staying fully invested at all times, such funds drooped in bear markets but soared in bull markets. Another answer could be that most of the older funds, good and bad, have disdained market-timing.

Not surprisingly, funds that claim they market-time, as a group, fared better than other funds during the October 1987 massacre.

The single fund that market-times most religiously may be Dreyfus Capital Value. Every single day, its managers decide whether stocks will go up or down, and invest accordingly — selling short or using leverage to buy. It's a fairly new fund, so its record doesn't prove much one way or another. But in 1987, when the Standard & Poor's 500 was up 5.2%, Dreyfus Capital Value was up 34.45%.

Most academicians scorn market-timing. Their studies show that, to make a profit as a market-timer, you must be right 70% to 80% of the time. Otherwise, trading commissions will decimate your returns. They have a point. A market-timer must make not one but two correct decisions: when to retreat to cash and when to jump back in.

But if you confine your investing to no-load mutual funds, you need not fret about commissions and sales charges. And if you are in only the most thrilling of bull markets, like the one of 1982-1987, and are on the sidelines only during the bloodiest of bear markets, like October 1987, you should do far better than any buy-and-holder.

The following funds did average or better in 1987, are highly rated by *Mutual Fund Values* for their long-term records, and are classified as market-timers by the *Handbook for No-Load Fund Investors*. All are no-load except Dreyfus Leverage (4.5%).

Fund	1987 Total Return	Telephone
Boston Company Managed Income	5.66	(800) 225-5267
Dreyfus Fund	8.21	(800) 645-6561
Dreyfus Leverage	11.24	(800) 645-6561
Founders Equity Income	1.96	(800) 525-2440
Gradison Established Growth	12.42	(800) 543-1818
IAI Regional	5.14	(612) 371-2884
IAI Stock	15.52	(612) 371-2884
Janus	4.20	(800) 525-3713
Janus Venture	5.15	(800) 525-3713
Lindner	8.83	(314) 727-5305
Mathers	27.04	(800) 962-3863
Partners	4.31	(800) 367-0770

Fund	1987 Total Return	Telephone
Scudder Growth and Income	3.54	(800) 225-2470
SteinRoe Special	4.27	(800) 338-2550
USAA Cornerstone	9.00	(800) 531-8000
USAA Mutual Income	3.43	(800) 531-8000
Valley Forge	4.83	(215) 688-6839

Certainly it should have been obvious that the market was overpriced in August and September of 1987. Price-earnings ratios were unusually high (22); dividends were unusually low (under 3%); the ratios of stock prices to book value were astounding—five and six to one for some blue-chip stocks, when one and a half or two is considered reasonable. It should have been equally clear that stocks were underpriced in 1973–1974, when price-earnings ratios were low, dividends were high, and price-to-book ratios were reasonable.

Even ordinary investors should be able to spot extreme market conditions—to lighten up when the market is reaching its all-time highs, and to load up when the market is in the doldrums. Not to practice a moderate version of market-timing, a moderate version of contrarianism, seems positively reckless. And, in practice, it's likely that the majority of successful, experienced investors—whatever they claim—practice a mild version of market-timing.

If volatility scares you, but you're tempted by the high returns of stock funds, you should certainly consider investing in one that market-times.

Among the newsletters that give market-timing advice are Fund Exchange, Seattle, Wash.; Zweig Forecast, New York City; Professional Tape Reader, Hollywood, Calif.; Stock-market Cycles, Los Angeles; Weber's Fund Advisor, New Hyde Park, N.Y.; Telephone Switch Newsletter, Huntington Beach, Calif.; No Load Fund*X, San Francisco; Mutual Fund Forecaster, Fort Lauderdale, Fla.; Growth Fund Guide, Rapid City, S.D.; Switch Fund Advisor, Rockville, Md.

You might write for sample copies, or read them in a large library.

48

FOLLOWING MOMENTUM

Individual stocks — and stock mutual funds — tend to have their ups and downs, depending on which business sectors, or which investment strategies, are in favor. Sometimes gold is up, technology down; sometimes basic-value investing is in vogue, sometimes buying growth companies.

To take advantage of this shifting tide, several money managers and newsletter writers recommend that investors keep switching into the hotter no-load funds and out of no-loads that have turned merely lukewarm. It is a cold-blooded approach. But cold-blooded investors generally seem to make the most money.

This strategy of "momentum-following" seems to work well in an ongoing bull market, but not necessarily in a bear market. For example, momentum-followers tended to be skewed toward volatile, fair-weather funds in October of 1987, and lost much if not all of the gains they made earlier in the year. Over the past few years, however, momentum-followers appear to have enjoyed unusually profitable returns.

Momentum-followers differ in just how they play follow-the-leader. Most of them put extra weight on mutual funds that have been excelling very recently — the last three months rather than the entire previous year, for example. One momentum-follower, Ken Weber, publisher of the Weber's Fund Advisor, shrewdly abandoned momentum-following just before the October crash. Now he's combined momentum-following with direct market-timing, using 39-week moving averages.

Newsletters that advocate momentum-following include Weber's Fund Advisor, P.O. Box 3490, New Hyde Park, N.Y. 11040; and No-Load Fund*X, 235 Montgomery St., San Francisco, Calif. 94104.

Some reservations: Obviously, momentum-following—if it's successful—will boost the amount of taxes you must pay soon, whereas someone who buys and holds can defer taxes longer.

A more important question is whether, over the long term, by switching from hot fund to hot fund, you will outperform a single fund's gifted portfolio manager. After all, any portfolio manager can also hopscotch from fashionable stock group to fashionable stock group—and, if his or her fund is fairly small, faster than you can by moving from fund to fund.

49

REDEMPTIONS

There are basically seven reasons to consider redeeming your shares:

1. The fund has underperformed similar funds.

A good guide, as mentioned earlier: if an aggressive-growth fund has underperformed similar funds for a year or two, or if a growth or growth-and-income fund has lagged behind similar funds for two or three years.

2. The successful portfolio manager has left.

If a fund is a member of a large, respectable family, it may not make much difference if a noted manager departs. The family can probably replace the departed with someone just as good. When an old-timer left Fidelity Puritan, to be replaced by young Richard Fentin, there was some nervousness among Puritan's shareholders. But Fentin has been an impressive manager. And Morris Smith seems to be following in Peter Lynch's footprints at Fidelity Magellan. On the other hand, T. Rowe Price Growth suffered badly when Price retired.

Of course, you may not know when a successful manager leaves. Some funds don't identify the names of their managers; others claim that they are run by a team of managers, not just one person. Still, the Securities and Exchange Commission is recommending that all funds identify their managers.

3. You need cash.

Perhaps there's another fund you want to invest in.

4. The fund's strategy changes.

If you have invested in a conservative fund, you might be somewhat aghast to find, from a quarterly report, that the fund is now investing in small-company stocks. And you might become worried if the manager announces that he or she is no longer looking for undervalued securities so much as growth stocks.

Even so, such changes may indicate that the manager is flexible — that he or she believes that small-company stocks are where the greater profits will be, or that the current fashion is growth stocks, not undervalued stocks.

5. When you have a loss.

See Key 50: TAXES.

6. When your financial situation changes.

You may want to sell aggressive-growth funds and move into income funds, for example, when you near retirement.

7. If the market seems poised to drop.

That brings us to the question of how to redeem your shares.

A fund must redeem your shares by 4 P.M. Eastern time on any trading day after it receives a proper request. The fund can borrow money, or use its cash reserves, to send you your money; it need not actually sell your share of the securities it owns. A fund must send you your money within seven calendar days of receiving proper forms.

Redemption Problems. Many shareholders, when they first invest in a fund, can choose to have telephone exchange or redemption privileges. But that may not help if the phone lines are tied up, or if it takes a while before a customer's representative answers. That happened on October 19, 1987, but it has happened at other times, too.

If you don't have telephone exchange or redemption privileges, you must send in a redemption letter, with your signature guaranteed by a commercial bank, a major brokerage firm, or maybe by a savings and loan association — not by a credit union or a notary public. A signature witnessed by a notary is not acceptable because the notary does not promise to make restitution if the signature turns out to be a forgery.

Another problem is that only about half of all funds now accept signatures guaranteed by S&Ls, though the percentage is increasing. Why the bias against savings and loans? One guess is that the funds' "transfer agents," who handle the paperwork, were once exclusively commercial banks, and they still remain prejudiced against S&Ls.

Most funds will redeem your shares upon a written request, without a signature guarantee—but only up to a certain amount. The amount depends on the particular fund. (With Fidelity funds, it's $25,000.) And some funds will not even reveal what amount of money they will redeem without a signature guarantee.

Here are some ways to get your money out of a fund quickly:

1. Buy into a fund that has a sister money-market fund and that offers a telephone-exchange privilege. That way, you can transfer your account from a stock or bond fund to the money-market fund quickly, and your money-market fund checks will give you access to your money in two or three days.

2. Buy into a fund that offers telephone redemption privileges. But only about 10% of all funds allow this, and usually with a limit—such as $5000.

3. Follow what the prospectus says about redemptions— even if you read nothing else in a prospectus. If the fund will redeem $5,000 worth of shares without a signature guarantee, and you want to redeem $9,800, send a letter one day redeeming $5,000, and a letter redeeming $4,800 the next. (It works.)

4. Buy into a fund that will wire redemptions to your bank. The redemption letter you send should include the bank's name, address, and "routing number" (phone the bank to find out), your account number, and whether the account is checking or savings. The charge is usually $10 or so.

5. Have a redemption letter ready in advance, with a signature guarantee. When you actually send the letter, you can add the date. A commercial bank where you have only a

safe-deposit box may guarantee your signature. If your bank is an S&L and your fund accepts a signature guarantee only from a commercial bank, ask your S&L whether it has a working relationship with a commercial bank that will, as a courtesy, process the guarantee. And while a stockbroker is supposed to watch you sign your name, many brokers will guarantee a signature even if you just mail in a letter.

6. Send your redemption letter by an overnight courier service, such as Federal Express, and ask the fund or its transfer agent to send your check by courier, too, billing you for the extra charge.

7. Open an account with discount broker Charles Schwab in San Francisco, and use its Mutual Fund Marketplace to sell your shares. Schwab has computerized links with many funds; with others, it knows whom to phone. Schwab buys and sells a variety of no-load funds for its customers, assessing a small charge.

A Standard Redemption Letter

Please redeem (number of shares) of my holdings in (name of fund). (Or: Please sell all my holdings in so-and-so fund.) My account number is (number).

Sell the shares I purchased on (date). (If you are not closing out your entire position, you may want to sell particular shares—those you bought most recently, if you want to lower your taxable gains; those you bought a while ago, if there is a fee levied when you redeem shares you bought recently.)

Please send a check for the amount to (your name and address).

Sincerely,
(your name as it appears on your mailings)

50

MINIMIZING TAXES

Of course, taxes should never dominate your investment decisions. But ...

• If you're thinking of buying a fund (A) with a front-end load, first buy a different fund (B) in the same family. Then sell Fund B, and put the balance in Fund A. You'll emerge with a quick tax deduction. Forget about it if Fund B has a redemption fee or if the two funds have different loads. But usually you can transfer within a family of funds without paying a sales commission. This tactic would be ideal for investing in a fund like Fidelity Capital Appreciation (3% load); you would first invest in, say, Fidelity Magellan (3% load, no redemption fee). You must wait 90 days before making such a transfer.

• Always be ready to sell a fund that has lost you money, and put the balance into a similar fund. If the fund you sold rebounds, your new fund is also likely to prosper; meanwhile, you have a tax deduction. Note that you cannot take a deduction on a security if you sell it, then buy a "substantially identical" security within 31 days after the sale — or within 31 days *before* the sale. But you can switch between mutual funds and not infringe this "wash sale" rule. Rarely are two funds substantially the same, even if one is supposedly a clone of the other. Nicholas and Nicholas II, for example, have very different holdings.

In fact, some clever investors buy two similar no-load

funds, then—before year's end—sell one if it has lost a sizable amount of money. They put the balance into the better-performing fund. They thus enjoy a tax deduction—and move their money over into a fund that's gaining altitude.

• If you want to reduce your holdings in a fund, sell the particular shares with the least gains—ordinarily, the ones you bought most recently. That will lower any taxes you owe for the current year. Of course, if you purchased shares, the fund plummeted, you bought more shares, and then the fund rebounded, you will realize less capital gains by selling the *older* shares.

If you have overall realized losses in your portfolio, you may again prefer to sell older shares, with greater gains, to offset those losses and perhaps wind up not owing any taxes at all. (You can offset losses against ordinary income, but only up to $3000 a year.)

Most funds don't send you certificates when you buy shares—unless you request them. So, to make sure the fund sells particular shares, specify—in your redemption letter—the date, price, or date *and* price at which you bought the shares you want to peddle.

• Don't buy shares of a stock fund, as mentioned earlier, just before a distribution. You'll promptly receive some of your investment back, and owe taxes on whatever dividends and capital gains the fund directs your way. Wait until after the fund's ex-dividend date to invest. Most stock funds make distributions in December, but check with the fund.

• If you have been reinvesting your distributions, be sure you use your various purchase prices as your "cost basis"—the cost of your investment in those shares—when you sell those shares and fill out your tax return. Don't make the mistake of using the net asset value of your first investment in the fund. Assuming that the fund's NAV has risen over the years, your new basis for extra shares will have been higher—and thus your profits will be lower, and so will any taxes you must pay.

• Don't forget to add to your cost basis any up-front sales charges you might have been assessed. (Any deferred sales charges or redemption fees you paid will have been subtracted from the amount you realized.)

• If you're thinking of investing in a mutual fund via a tax-sheltered plan—an IRA, an HR-10 (Keogh) plan, 401 (k) plan, a variable insurance contract, a variable annuity—bear in mind that you usually cannot deduct any losses you may incur. For tax-sheltered arrangements, consider investing in an income mutual fund or any very conservative fund, then investing in volatile funds for your personal portfolio. That way, you have the option of taking tax-deductible losses.

On the other hand, volatile funds may bless you with the highest capital gains, and capital gains are now taxed just like ordinary income. So you might want to consider an aggressive-growth fund for a tax-sheltered plan if you plan to hold on to it through thick and thin—and you're confident that the fund you choose will excel in bull markets, even if it takes a dive in down markets.

There *is* a way to take a loss on a fund in a tax-sheltered plan, like an IRA. You can make a premature withdrawal. You will pay a tax penalty, of course—unless you're over $59^1/2$, or disabled, or you withdraw the money in accordance with your estimated life-span (in other words, as an annuity). But if you withdraw from an IRA in the same year you opened it, you will incur a tax penalty only on any income you've received, not on both your income and your contribution. Compare the size of your tax-deductible loss against the tax penalty.

• If you own shares of a fund that buys Treasury obligations, check with your state tax department to learn whether the income you received from that fund is exempt from state taxes. Some states say yes, others say no.

• For guidance in filling out your tax return, ask the Internal Revenue Service for Publication 564 (Mutual Fund Distributions).

TEN KEY DECISIONS
YOU MUST MAKE

1. Do you want a stockbroker or financial planner to buy funds for you?

If your answer is yes, choose a load fund. If you want to invest on your own and save on commission costs, choose a no-load or low-load fund. (Note: All money market funds are no-loads.)

2. Do you want a fund that gives you regular income, or one that may give you even more of a profit, with capital gains?

For income, choose a fixed-income or money-market fund. For possibly greater profit, an equities (stock) fund. For a combination, choose a balanced or stock income fund.

3. What kind of stock fund do you want?

You can choose among many classifications—among them, aggressive, growth, growth and income, and stock income. Your decision will depend on how much volatility and risk you can stand—and how much income you may need.

4. Do you want an all-weather, a fair-weather, or a foul-weather stock fund?

All-weather funds do respectably in both up markets and down markets; fair-weather funds excel in up markets; foul-weather funds do best in down markets.

5. What kind of investment strategy do you favor?

Buying stocks whose earnings are climbing and whose prices rising? Stocks of companies that are growing? Under-valued stocks? Stocks of companies that may benefit because of special situations? Or just index funds stocks that will do about as well as the general market? Choose your funds accordingly.

6. Do you want a fund that market-times?

A fund that practices market-timing—buying or selling depending on the direction of the market—may keep you from losing money in bear markets but may also cause you to miss out on bull markets.

7. Do you want a specialty/sector fund?

You can choose funds that concentrate in a particular industry, like health care, real estate, precious metals, or utilities, or in one part of the United States or one foreign country.

8. What kind of fixed-income fund do you want?

All Treasurys? Treasurys plus mortgage securities backed by the government? Or just mortgage securities? High-grade corporates or high-yield corporates? High-grade municipals or high-yield municipals? International bonds? Short-term, intermediate-term, or long-term? Your decisions will depend on how high a yield you want, and how much risk you can live with.

9. Do you want a fund from a family or a stand-alone fund?

A family is usually more convenient — but don't choose a family member over a similar stand-alone fund with a better record.

10. Once you know the kind of fund you want, how do you find out which funds in that category have the best performance records and the fewest handicaps?

Read this book, giving particular attention to the successful funds listed in many of the keys.

QUESTIONS AND ANSWERS

1. Can you define "mutual fund" in plain English?

When investors pool their money to buy securities, you have a mutual fund. With a large sum, the group can purchase a wide variety of stocks or bonds. The individual investor owns shares of all these securities, in proportion to the money he or she has contributed.

Usually the term "mutual fund" also means the sort of investment company that lets you buy and sell shares directly from the fund. (If the shareholders buy and sell shares from other shareholders, it's a "closed-end" mutual fund.) The term also usually means a company that actively buys and sells securities. (If the securities in the fund aren't traded, but are simply held in the fund for years, it's a "unit investment trust.")

Finally, many people use the term "mutual fund" to mean an investment company that concentrates on buying and selling stocks — not bonds or short-term debt instruments (a money market fund).

2. Why shouldn't I just buy and sell stocks on my own?

With a mutual fund, you can get an enormous basketful of different stocks for a comparatively small amount of money. For $2500 (the minimum first investment), you could buy shares of Fidelity Magellan, for example. That fund owns about 650 different stocks. And with such diversity, you are purchasing a large measure of safety. One poorly chosen stock won't lay you low.

Besides, with a fund you would have an expert making the decisions about what to buy and sell — and when. In the case of Fidelity Magellan, it's now a fellow named Morris Smith. If you had put money in Magellan in 1981, in ten years it would have grown 21.81% a year.

3. Why shouldn't I just keep all my money in bank CDs? I won't lose a cent that way, and I won't have to become an investment expert.

With a CD, over the years you would be lucky if your money earned more than the inflation rate. You could be losing money and not know it.

But history has shown that the return from stocks outperforms the inflation rate. Of course, you'll have to choose the right stocks or mutual funds, and be prepared for ups and downs in the value of your investment.

4. I know lots of people who have lost money buying mutual funds. Why should I buy any?

Actually, hardly anyone has lost money in mutual funds who has bought a fund with a good track record, then held on for several years. Of course, people have lost money in funds. But typically they bought when the stock market was high and then sold when the prices went down.

The average stock fund has returned an average of 9% to 10% a year over the years — far better than fixed-interest investments like CDs. The better funds have returned 15% to 20%.

If you want to raise the odds against your losing money in a stock fund, even temporarily, buy a fund that owns bonds as well as stocks — a balanced fund. Or a fund that may buy real estate stocks or precious metals stocks as well — an asset-allocation fund. Or an index fund, which virtually mimics the performance of a market index, like the Standard & Poor's 500.

Or invest in a fund gradually — a set amount every month, every three months, or every six months. That way, you'll help make sure that the prices you pay for a fund's shares are average prices, not unusually high prices.

5. How much money might I make in one year by buying a mutual fund?

The record seems to be about 184% of the original investment. But in recent years 10% to 15% has been average.

6. How much would I have lost in 1987, because of the crash?

Bear in mind that, before October 19, 1987, the stock market had been going up and up. Overall, the Standard & Poor's 500 gained 5.2% in 1987. Most funds made less than that, and some did lose money.

Despite 1987, the average stock fund was up around 10% a year for the three-year period 1985–1987.

7. Where can I go to get advice about buying funds?

You can ask a stockbroker or financial planner.

But buying good funds isn't hard. You can do it on your own. You'll save money. You won't have to pay anyone a fee, and a commission won't be deducted from your investment money. You yourself may also do as good a job as anyone else.

8. Can I get taken by buying mutual funds?

Yes.

You could buy funds that have done poorly in the past—and therefore may do poorly in the future. In fact, some stockbrokers and financial planners may urge you to buy funds with dreadful records, just because they themselves receive sizable commissions from those funds.

You can avoid bad funds (a) by buying funds on your own, funds that don't pay salespeople commissions ("no-loads"), and (b) by checking that any fund you buy has done better than similar funds over the past three to five years.

9. Can you give me the names of three no-load funds with good three-to-five-year records?

Janus, Lindner, and Wellesley Income. For the latest information on which funds are doing well, check one of the reference books named in the Introduction.

10. Is that all there is to it?
No.
You should know a good deal about any fund before you buy shares. For example, some funds don't fare as well as most other funds in a bull market. They may own many bonds as well as stocks. Others may be exceptionally poor performers in bear markets.

Telephone the funds of your choice and ask for a prospectus and an application form. Read as much of each prospectus as you can manage, then consult other sources of information, like the *Mutual Fund Sourcebook*. And check various newsletters.

11. How can I tell that a fund is worth buying?
Your single most important guide is that it has a good record — over three years, five years, ten years (if it's been in existence that long).

Examine other criteria as well, such as whether a fund has a high sales charge, a high expense ratio, or unusually high volatility; whether the current portfolio manager is the same person who was responsible for the fund's excellent performance in the past; whether the fund is part of a respected family of funds.

But the fund's track record should be your chief guide.

12. Aren't mutual funds confusing?
They can be, if you try to learn everything about them all at once.

The problem is that you have so many choices. But take it slowly, step by step, and you won't feel overwhelmed.

You can stick to simple choices when you begin investing — balanced funds like Wellington, for example, or growth and income funds like Mutual Qualified.

And, as you go along, you can add to your knowledge, a little bit at a time.

13. I want to make a big profit quickly, but I don't want much risk. What should I do?

When you find out, let me know.

14. Is it true that, over the long term, all funds perform about the same?

No.

A few academics claim that the number of funds that do better than average, or worse than average, are just what you would expect by chance. This is merely suggestive; it's not proof. But one academic has gone so far as to argue that people should choose funds randomly, just by throwing darts at a list of fund names.

The fact is that some funds, year after year, do perform well. Others perform abysmally, year after year. And it tends to be the star performers whose managers have clear and logical investment philosophies, while the poor performers have managers whose philosophies are vague and amorphous.

Anyone who thinks chance governs mutual fund performance might logically buy one of the notorious Steadman funds, which have lost money in recent years, and avoid Fidelity Magellan, Mutual Shares, Windsor, SoGen International, and other stars in the mutual-fund firmament.

15. I just want to get my feet wet buying mutual funds. Can you name one fund for me to buy?

If you don't already have a money market mutual fund, you could start that way. All families of funds — Vanguard, Fidelity, 20th Century, Strong, and so forth — offer money market funds. Such a fund is like a fancy checking account. You get higher interest, but your checks usually must be for at least $250 or $500.

For a stock fund, your safest choice may be Valley Forge. It's a fund that occasionally buys blue-chip stock at market lows, generally making a quick killing, before it retreats back into cash. After owning its shares for a while, though, you may yearn for a little excitement.

16. What are the most common mistakes that beginning investors in mutual funds make?

The two most common mistakes may be:

(a) Selling funds too soon. Too many people buy shares, watch the fund's price per share sink (perhaps along with the stock market as a whole), then sell out. You should give any fund you buy a decent chance.

(b) Not selling funds soon enough. As a rough rule, if a fund you've bought has underperformed similar funds for a year or two, it's time to replace it. Another alternative is to sell any fund you own that can give you a sizable tax loss, then put the balance into a similar fund with a good record.

17. I just want income — I'm retired. Should I buy mutual funds?

Certainly. You can buy a variety of funds composed of all sorts of fixed-income obligations — U.S. Treasury securities, Ginnie Maes, corporate bonds, municipal bonds, and so forth. Such funds will give you diversification and a manager who, ideally, knows not only how to buy obligations whose return matches their risk, but also when to buy long-term obligations and when to buy short-term obligations. The Vanguard family offers all sorts of fixed-income funds, with no sales charges and with low expenses.

18. How many different funds should I own?

No one really knows, but 10 to 15 is common.

You don't want many different funds in retirement accounts, because each fund will levy its own yearly fee. And you certainly don't want many funds that have sales charges if, by combining your investments, you could have gotten a reduction in the charge. (Sometimes you can get a break if you invest over $10,000 or $25,000.) And you don't want to own so many funds that you can't keep track of them.

Still, it makes sense to own shares of a variety of funds that practice different investment strategies — and even to own shares of funds that seem pretty much alike, just to hedge your bets.

19. What sort of investor shouldn't buy mutual funds?

Someone so wealthy that he or she can hire a top-flight money manager directly, and get individual attention. Money managers tend to pay special attention to investors with $500,000 or more.

20. What are the drawbacks of mutual funds?

One of them is that you must sometimes make difficult decisions. For example, few if any funds have unblemished records. A fund that hasn't had a poor year would probably have so much money pouring in from investors that its directors would be forced to close its doors to new investors. What if one of the funds you hold doesn't do well one year? Should you count on its rebounding—or might the fund continue to do poorly year after year? Your safest course isn't to wait around to find out. Switch to a similar fund that has been doing better recently.

Another drawback is the difficulty of determining whether a fund really has a good record. What if it has done well for the past year, but just average for the five years before that? What if it performed spectacularly for five years, then did poorly last year?

In such cases you'll have to use your own judgment. But experts suggest emphasizing a fund's three- and five-year records. Don't buy shares of a 90-day wonder; don't buy shares of a fund whose glory days were eight, nine, or ten years ago.

Still another drawback is that funds buy and sell securities; few of them buy and hold. That means that you will have to pay more taxes—and sooner—on your gains from a mutual fund than if you had bought stocks on your own and just hung on. It can be especially annoying to own shares of a fund that has lost you money—yet you've paid taxes on the "gains" the fund has distributed to you.

Ideally, despite your having paid taxes sooner with a fund, you've reaped more gains than you would have on your own. Of course, you needn't worry about this drawback if your funds are in a tax-deferred retirement account.

GLOSSARY

Adviser   A company that a mutual fund employs to manage the fund's investments.

Asking (offering) price   Price per share of a mutual fund (*see* net asset value), plus sales charges. For funds with no front-end sales charge, the asking price is the same as the net asset value.

Aggressive growth fund   A fund that seeks maximum capital gains. It usually remains fully invested in stocks at all times; it buys small, speculative companies and depressed stocks; and it may employ techniques like selling short and using leverage. Aggressive growth funds tend to be especially volatile.

All-weather fund   A fund that does well in bull and bear markets.

Alpha   Number that measures how well a fund has performed, considering its volatility. An alpha above 0 is considered desirable.

Appreciation   Growth in value of an asset.

Asset allocation fund   A fund that either keeps a fixed percentage of its assets in various instruments—bonds, stocks, precious-metals stocks, real-estate stocks—or varies the percentages, depending on where the fund managers think the investment markets are heading. A true asset-allocation fund has some investments in inflation-resistant hard assets (precious metals, real estate).

Automatic reinvestment Choice a shareholder can make to have distributions or dividends reinvested in more fund shares.

Bear market Time when stocks (or other investments) keep sinking in value, despite occasional rallies, or when stocks remain at depressed levels.

Beta coefficient Number that measures how volatile a stock or a mutual fund is. The Standard & Poor's 500 is given a beta of 1. A stock or fund with a beta of 1.20 bobs up and down 20% more; a stock or fund with a beta of 0.80 bobs up and down 20% less. Beta is sometimes equated with riskiness.

Back-end load A charge when you sell shares of certain mutual funds. Also called a deferred sales charge.

Balanced fund A fund that invests in both stocks and bonds—typically 60% in bonds, 40% in stocks.

Basic value investing Investment strategy that concentrates on buying seemingly undervalued stocks, based on their price-earnings ratio, price to book value, and other indicators.

Basis point In bond yields, 0.01%. If a bond's yield goes from 10% to 11%, it has increased by 100 basis points.

Bid or **Sell price** Price at which a mutual fund's shares are bought back by the fund. The bid price usually is the current net asset value per share—unless there's a redemption fee or back-end load.

Blue chip Stock of a large, prosperous, well-established company. The 30 stocks in the Dow Jones Industrial Average—including IBM, AT&T, Exxon—are unquestionably blue chips.

Blue-sky law Legislation passed by individual states to protect investors. (A judge once said that one stock offering had the value of a patch of blue sky.)

Bond A debt instrument that pays a regular interest, whether or not the company issuing the bond is making money. Debt instruments are "senior" securities: Their holders must be paid before a company pays owners of its stock.

Bond fund A fund that invests mainly in corporate, municipal, U.S. Treasury securities. Such a fund emphasizes income rather than capital gains.

Bond rating System of grading bonds on their ability to pay their obligations. Standard & Poor's ratings range from AAA (extremely unlikely to default) to D (in default). Moody's ratings are similar.

Book value Total value of a company's assets minus its liabilities, as carried on the balance sheet.

Bottom up Method of investing in which the investor concentrates on buying attractive stocks, whatever the broad trends of the market or the economy.

Broker/dealer Firm, like Merrill Lynch, that buys and sells load mutual funds and other securities to the public.

Bull market Time when stocks (or other securities) keep climbing in value, despite occasional stumbles. Sometimes the boundary between bull and bear markets isn't sharp.

Bullion Gold or silver in bars or ingots, not as coins.

Buy and hold Investment strategy that entails buying shares of stock or a mutual fund for the long term and selling them only in special circumstances, such as after a long-term loss.

Callable Bond that can be paid off by the issuing company before its scheduled maturity.

Cash equivalents Short-term obligations, like Treasury bills.

Clone fund A fund that imitates another fund, which may have become excessively large.

Closed fund A fund that has stopped issuing new shares. Funds close either because they are so large that the managers cannot find enough good investments, or because the manager prefers investing only in small companies, and cannot cope with large amounts of money.

Closed-end investment company A mutual fund whose shares are bought and sold on an exchange or over-the-counter, by investors trading among themselves. A closed-end fund issues only a limited number of shares. *See* open-end investment company.

Commercial paper Short-term notes, issued by corporations, banks, or government agencies.

Common stock Security representing ownership of a public corporation's assets.

Consumer price index Measure of the changes in prices to retail purchasers, as calculated by the Bureau of Labor Statistics.

Contrarian investing Buying securities cheaply when other investors are pessimistic, selling securities dearly when other investors are optimistic.

Conversion privilege Right of a shareholder to switch from one fund in a family to another.

Convertible securities Preferred stock or bond that can be exchanged for another security under certain circumstances.

Current yield Dividends paid to investors, as a percentage of the current price.

Custodian Bank or other institution that stores the securities of a mutual fund.

Date of record Date on which all investors in a security or fund become entitled to receive interest or dividends.

Deferred sales charge Sales charge you pay when you sell the shares of a load fund.

Distributions Payments that a mutual fund makes to its shareholders, from the sales of its securities, from interest, from dividends or a return of the shareholder's original investment.

Distributor Company that buys shares of a mutual fund and helps sell them to the public.

Diversification Spreading investments over a variety of different securities, to reduce risk.

Diversified investment company Company whose investments are limited to no more than 5% in a single issue, and no more than 10% of that issuer's outstanding securities; at least 75% of its assets must be in varied securities.

Dividends Money (or stock) that a company pays the owners of its stock, usually four times a year.

Dollar-cost averaging Investing the same amount of money at regular intervals, so that when securities are low-priced you buy more shares. A method of diversifying the prices at which you buy securities.

Dow Jones Industrial Average   Model for the stock market as a whole. It consists of 30 blue-chip stocks.

Efficient market   Theory that all securities are properly priced, and investors will do better than average only in proportion to the extra risks they take.

Equities   Stocks, real estate, other assets that an investor owns, as opposed to bonds, where an investor lends money.

Equity REIT   A real estate investment trust that concentrates on buying shares of real estate companies. *See* Mortgage REIT.

Eurodollars   U.S. currency held in foreign banks.

Event risk   The danger that a bond will lose value because of special situations, such as the issuer being subject to a leveraged buyout and acquiring a great deal of new debt.

Ex dividend   The time between the announcement of a dividend and the actual payment. During this time, new investors are not entitled to the dividend. *See* Ex distribution.

Ex distribution   The date on which distributions from a mutual fund are deducted from its assets. Also called ex dividend.

Exchange privilege   *See* conversion privilege.

Expense ratio   Measure of a fund's efficiency in keeping costs down. Annual expenses are divided by average net assets, to factor in economies of scale. Even so, large funds usually have lower expense ratios than small funds.

Fair-weather fund   A fund that excels in bull markets but gives a mediocre or poor performance in bear markets.

Fixed-income fund   A fund that invests mainly in bonds and preferred stock.

Family   Group of mutual funds under one umbrella, typically consisting of a stock bond, a bond fund, and a money-market fund.

Formula investing   Investing according to mechanical techniques, such as dollar-cost averaging.

Foul-weather fund   A fund that excels in bear markets, one explanation being that the fund invests in securities that are already undervalued.

Front-end load   Sales commission investors pay at the time they buy shares of a mutual fund.

GNMA fund   A fund that invests in mortgage securities issued by the Government National Mortgage Association.

Global fund   A fund that invests in both U.S. and foreign securities.

Growth fund   A fund that invests in small companies that seem to have bright futures.

Hedge fund   A fund that not only invests in securities, but may also sell short or write options, in order to protect iself from losses.

Income fund   A fund that stresses current income rather than growth of capital. Such funds may be mainly invested in high-yielding stocks or in bonds.

Index   Model of an investment market—stocks, bonds, utilities, health-care stocks, and so forth.

Index fund   A fund that attempts to emulate the performance of an index, like the Standard & Poor's 500 or the Shearson-Lehman Bond Index.

Initial public offering   Corporation's initial offering of stock to the public. While many stock prices then proceed to rise, others sink—expecially the IPOs or closed-end investment companies.

Institutional investor   Pension fund, bank, mutual fund, or other huge investor. Today they dominate the stock market.

International fund   A fund that invests in the securities of foreign corporations or governments.

Investment objective   Goals of a mutual fund, such as long-term capital gains, with income secondary.

Investment grade bonds   Bonds rated BBB, Standard & Poor's fourth-highest category, and above.

Junk bonds   Bonds rated BB or below by Standard & Poor's. Such bonds are not so safe as investment grade bonds, but they pay higher interest. Also called "high yield" bonds.

Leverage   Buying stocks or other securities by borrowing money.

Leveraged buyout   Buyout of a company from its stock-holders, with the new owners borrowing funds to pay for the purchase, and perhaps saddling the new company with new debt.

Limited partnership   Investment group made up of a general partner, who manages a project, and the limited partners, who invest money and whose liability is limited.

Liquidity   Measure of how readily an asset can be sold for cash. If an asset can readily be sold, but at a loss, its liquidity is compromised. In this respect, a money-market fund is far more liquid than a stock fund.

Load   Commission charge that buyers of certain mutual funds must pay. The load goes to the stockbroker and the distributor, or—in the case of most low-load funds—to the fund itself. Generally, low-load funds charge 1%-3%; medium loads, 3%-6%; full loads, 6%-8.5%. No-load funds sell their shares directly to investors.

Management company   Investment company that runs a mutual fund.

Management fee   Money that a mutual fund pays its investment adviser; usually 1/2% to 1% of the fund's net assets.

Market timing   Attempting to buy securities near the end of a bear market, and to sell them near the end of a bull market—in other words, to buy low and sell high. *See* Market timing.

Maturity   When a loan—or a bond—is due to be paid off by the debtor or by the issuing company.

Momentum following   Buying funds or stocks that have been excelling, and selling those that are faltering.

Money-market fund   A fund that invests in debt obligations with maturities of no more than a year. To keep the principal unchanging, usually at $1 a share, the fund varies the yield. Banks' funds are called money market deposit accounts.

Mortgage-backed securities   Shares of a pool of mortgages, issued by Fannie Mae (Federal National Mortgage Association), Freddie Mac (Federal Home Loan Mortgage Corporation), or Ginnie Mae (Government National Mortgage Association). Investors receive regular payments of principal and interest from the underlying mortgages.

Mortgage REIT Real estate investment trust that concentrates on lending money to builders and buyers. *See* Equity REIT.

Moving averages Average price of securities, over a few days or several years. The general direction of prices is a key guide used by market timers.

Municipal bond fund A fund that invests in tax-exempt bonds issued by states, cities, and local governments. The bonds may be short, intermediate, or long term, and they may be high rated or low rated.

NASDAQ National Association of Securities Dealers Automated Quotations, a group that provides quotations on over-the-counter securities and on mutual funds.

NASD National Association of Securities Dealers, the group that policies Securities and Exchange Commission rules governing mutual funds and over-the-counter securities.

Net assets Value of a fund's holdings, minus debts, such as taxes owed.

Net asset value Price per share of a fund: net assets divided by number of shares outstanding.

No-load A fund that does not charge a front-end commission. A "pure" no-load also has no deferred sales charge, and typically no redemption fee and no 12b-1 fee.

Offering price *See* Asking price.

Open-end investment company A fund that can continually issue more shares and thus add to its net assets. *See* Closed-end investment company.

Option The right to buy or sell securities at certain prices. A call option gives the buyer the right to buy 100 shares of a specified security at a set price before a specific date—usually 3, 6, or 9 months; a put option, to sell the shares in the same manner. Most buyers of calls think the market is going up; most buyers of puts think the market is going down.

Over-the-counter Market in which securities are bought and sold through dealers, not on the floor of an exchange. OTC stocks are typically those of smaller companies.

Payment date The date when a mutual fund makes distributions. It is usually a few days after the date of record, when distributions are set aside from assets.

Performance How well a fund has fared over a certain time period, usually measured by capital gains, dividends, and interest the fund has earned.

Portfolio Various securities held by an individual or a fund.

Portfolio manager Person or committee that makes buy-and-sell decisions for a fund.

Preferred stock Security that pays a fixed return, and whose holders must be paid before the holders of common stock.

Premium Percentage that a security's price exceeds its net asset value per share. A bond paying high interest may trade at a premium.

Price-earnings ratio. Price per share of a stock, divided by its last 12 months of earnings (or estimated earnings for the next year). The p/e ratio indicates how popular a stock is by reflecting how much investors are willing to pay for its earning power.

Prospectus Official document describing a mutual fund. It must be furnished to investors.

Quotation Highest bid and lowest offer on a security.

Random walk The theory that stock prices are unpredictable.

Real estate investment trust Company that buys real estate, lends money to real estate companies, or both. Usually a REIT's shares are publicly traded.

Redemption fee Charge a fund may levy, especially if an investor sells shares purchased recently.

Risk Either the volatility of an investment, or the possibility that the investment will lose value.

Risk tolerance Ability of a person to accept what may be temporary losses from an investment.

Sales charge Commission an investor must pay to buy shares of certain load mutual funds or of a limited partnership.

Sector Stocks in one industry.

Secular Long-term.

Securities Stocks, bonds, options, warrants, or other instruments, that signify a corporation's obligations to a investor.

Securities and Exchange Commission (SEC) Federal agency, created in 1934, that administers the securities laws.

Sell short To borrow a security through a broker, sell it, and buy it back later. Short sellers expect a security's price to decline.

Series fund A fund with more than one portfolio.

Signature guarantee Document in which an investor's signature is warranted as authentic. Signature guarantees may be required before a shareholder can redeem mutual fund shares. The guarantee usually must be made by a commercial bank or national brokerage firm, not by a notary.

Special situation Stock that is expected to benefit from a new development, such as an important new product or management change.

Spread Difference between the bid and the offer prices on a stock or bond.

Standard & Poor's 500 Popular replica of the stock market as a whole, based on the prices of 500 widely held common stocks.

Standard deviation Volatility of an investment, measured by comparing its average price with the degree of its ups and downs.

Top down Method of investing in which the investor looks at general economic trends, then decides which industries and companies will benefit. *See* Bottom up.

Total return Profit or loss that a mutual fund has achieved over a period of time, including capital gains or losses, interest and dividends, and expenses. It is expressed as a percentage of the original value of the assets.

Transfer agent Company hired by a mutual fund to handle its paperwork.

Treasury Debts of the U.S. Government. The maturities of Treasury bills are up to one year, of notes, two to ten years, and of bonds, ten to thirty years.

Turnover ratio   Trading activity of a mutual fund, calculated by dividing the lesser of purchases or sales for the fund's fiscal year by the monthly average of the portfolio's net assets. Excluded are securities that mature within a year. A turnover ratio of 100% is the equivalent of a complete portfolio turnover.

12b-1 fee   Amount that a fund takes from its assets—and thus from its shareholders—to pay for distribution and marketing costs. Usually .25% to 1.25% of assets. Also called a hidden load.

Unit investment trust   A fund that buys a portfolio of securities—usually bonds—and normally holds them until maturity.

Volatility   Fluctuations in the price of a security or index of securities.

Wilshire 5000   Model of all stocks, including those on the New York Stock Exchange, the American Exchange, and over-the-counter. The Wilshire is one of the broadest indexes, and includes over 6,000 stocks.

Yield   Regular income from a fund, expressed as a percentage of the fund's average net asset value, not including capital gains or losses.

Yield to maturity   Yield (as above) plus any certain gains or loss on the price of a bond from now until the time it comes due, expressed as a percentage of the bond's price.

Yield curve   Graph comparing the interest rates of similar bonds according to their maturities. Usually long-term rates are higher than short-term rates. When short-term rates are higher, it is a negative yield curver.

Zero coupon bond   A bond sold at a small fraction of its face value. It gradually appreciates, but no interest is paid to investors, who must nonetheless pay taxes on the interest (except for tax-exempt bonds). Earnings accumulate until maturity.

INDEX

155

157

BARRON'S BUSINESS KEYS Each "key" explains approximately 50 concepts and provides a glossary and index. Each book: Paperback, 160 pp., 4 3/16" x 7", $4.95, Can. $6.50. ISBN Prefix: 0-8120.

Available at bookstores, or by mail from Barron's. Enclose check or money order for full amount plus sales tax where applicable and 10% for postage & handling (minimum charge $3.75, Can. $4.00) Prices subject to change without notice.

Barron's Educational Series, Inc. • 250 Wireless Blvd.
Hauppauge, NY 11788 • Call toll-free: 1-800-645-3476
In Canada: Georgetown Book Warehouse
34 Armstrong Ave., Georgetown, Ont. L7G 4R9
Call toll-free: 1-800-247-7160   R 5/94

More selected BARRON'S titles:

DICTIONARY OF ACCOUNTING TERMS
Siegel and Shim
Nearly 2500 terms related to accounting are defined.
Paperback, $10.95, Can. $14.50 (3766-9)

DICTIONARY OF MARKETING TERMS
Imber and Toffler
Nearly 3000 terms used in the marketing and ad industry are defined.
Paperback, $11.95, Can. $15.95 (1783-8)

DICTIONARY OF BANKING TERMS
Fitch
Nearly 3000 terms related to banking, finance and money management.
Paperback, $10.95, Can. $14.50 (3946-7)

DICTIONARY OF BUSINESS TERMS, 2nd EDITION
Friedman, general editor
Over 6000 entries define business terms.
Paperback, $11.95, Can. $15.95 (1530-4)

BARRON'S BUSINESS REVIEW SERIES
These guides explain topics covered in a college level business course.
Each book: paperback
ACCOUNTING, 2nd EDITION. *Eisen.* $11.95,Can.$15.95 (4375 8)
BUSINESS LAW, 2nd EDITION. *Hardwicke and Emerson.* $11.95, Can. $15.95 (1385 9)
BUSINESS STATISTICS, 2nd EDITION. *Downing and Clark.* $11.95, Can. $15.95 (1384-0)
ECONOMICS, 2nd EDITION. *Wessels.* $11.95, Can. $15.95 (1392 1)
FINANCE, 2ndEDITION. *Groppelli and Nikbakht.* $11.95, Can. $15.95 (4373 1)
MANAGEMENT, 2nd EDITION. *Montana and Chanulv.* $11.95, Can. $15.95 (1549 5)
MARKETING, 2nd EDITION. *Sandhusen.* $11.95, Can. $15.95 (1548-7)
QUANTITATIVE METHODS. *Downing and Clark.* $10.95, Can. $14.95 (3947 5)

BARRON'S FOREIGN LANGUAGE BUSINESS DICTIONARIES
Six bilingual dictionaries translate about 3000 terms not found in most foreign phrasebooks:
Each book, paperback: $9.95, Can. $11.95
FRENCH FOR THE BUSINESS TRAVELER, ISBN 1768-4
GERMAN FOR THE BUSINESS TRAVELER, ISBN 1769-2
ITALIAN FOR THE BUSINESS TRAVELER, ISBN 1771-4
KOREAN FOR THE BUSINESS TRAVELER, ISBN 1772-2
RUSSIAN FOR THE BUSINESS TRAVELER, ISBN 1784-6
SPANISH FOR THE BUSINESS TRAVELER, ISBN 1773-0
All prices are in U.S. and Canadian dollars and subject to change without notice.
At your bookseller, or order direct adding 10% postage (rninumum charge $3.75, Canada $4.00) N.Y. residents add sales tax.   ISBN PREFIX 0-8120

Barron's Educational Series, Inc.
250 Wireless Boulevard, Hauppauge, NY 11788
Call toll-free: 1.800.645.3476
In Canada: Georgetown Book Warehouse
34 Armstrong Ave., Georgetown, Ontario L7G 4R9
Call toll-free: 1-800-247-7160